The Meditation Guidebook for Beginners

A Mindfulness Meditation Workbook

Book 3 of the Mind Improvement for Beginners Series

Dane Krauss

Text Copyright © Dane Krauss

All rights reserved. No part of this guide may be reproduced in any form without permission in writing from the publisher except in the case of brief quotations embodied in critical articles or reviews.

Legal & Disclaimer

The information contained in this book and its contents is not designed to replace or take the place of any form of medical or professional advice; and is not meant to replace the need for independent medical, financial, legal or other professional advice or services, as may be required. The content and information in this book have been provided for educational and entertainment purposes only.

The content and information contained in this book has been compiled from sources deemed reliable, and it is accurate to the best of the Author's knowledge, information and belief. However, the Author cannot guarantee its accuracy and validity and cannot be held liable for any errors and/or omissions. Further, changes are periodically made to this book as and when needed. Where appropriate and/or necessary, you must consult a professional (including but not limited to your doctor, attorney, financial advisor or such other professional advisor) before using any of the suggested remedies, techniques, or information in this book.

Upon using the contents and information contained in this book, you agree to hold harmless the Author from and against any damages, costs, and expenses, including any legal fees potentially resulting from the application of any of the information provided by this book. This disclaimer applies to any loss, damages or injury caused by the use and application, whether directly or indirectly, of any advice or information presented, whether for breach of contract, tort, negligence, personal injury, criminal intent, or under any other cause of action.

You agree to accept all risks of using the information presented inside this book.

You agree that by continuing to read this book, where appropriate and/or necessary, you shall consult a professional (including but not limited to your doctor, attorney, or financial advisor or such other advisor as needed) before using any of the suggested remedies, techniques, or information in this book.

THE MEDITATION GUIDEBOOK FOR BEGINNERS

Introduction 6

Chapter 1: The History of Meditation 10

Chapter 2: Benefits of Meditation for the Body, Mind, and Soul 31

Chapter 3: The Different Concepts of Meditation 41

Chapter 4: Meditation Posture 67

Chapter 5: Meditation for the Body Chakra 77

Chapter 6: The Art of Aura Meditation – An Exercise 96

Chapter 7: Where to Meditate 104

Chapter 8: When to Meditate 118

Chapter 9: Daily Meditation Worksheets 125

Chapter 10: Taking the Edginess Off in the Modern Day 143

Chapter 11: Making Meditation a Daily Habit 152

Chapter 12: The Obstacles and how to Best Prepare Yourself 158

Chapter 13: The Future Of Meditation 169

Conclusion 172

Check Out Other Books 175

Bonus Free Material 177

Introduction

The ability to keep a sense of calm amidst a world full of noise is becoming more and more difficult to achieve. It takes a great deal to master calm despite our busy and impossible schedules, unending demands, and too many responsibilities. Because of this, techniques are employed to take your mind from chaos to calmness. Just like taking a nice warm shower cleanses our bodies, we need to detoxify and cleanse our minds as often and as consistently as we can. This can increase our capacity for well-being, love, happiness, and creativity.

Meditation is a habitual process that enables one to train his mind to focus and redirect thoughts. You can do this in order to affect changes within your internal self, promoting positive changes in both your mind and body. When an active mind and quiet mind are combined, this can provide the best formula for living a harmonious life with clarity towards your surroundings. One can better explore the world more clearly and move forward to make changes in their life in accordance to their will.

More and more these days we see countless recommendations to practice the age old art and science of meditation. Most, if not all, extol its seemingly magical power on the human psyche through its purported benefits. These recommendations and claims have stood the test of time- they are universally accepted and well justified. For eons past those who came before us have spoken volumes regarding this great gift we all posses, but today sometimes, we neglect to use. Why now are we again reminded of this?

All of us are participating either aware or unaware in a quantum shift bringing at times, tumultuous changes in all areas of our society and world structures. No one is exempt from the effects these rapid changes bring. While universally experienced, these trans-formative energies are individually unique and processed differently depending on a person's outlook.

With a little discipline and practice we can apply this gift of meditation to help balance stress levels, reduce mind-movies which seem to play nonstop to bring increasing levels of joy, clarity and purpose into life.

While it's true that meditative practices are known by many names in virtually all cultures each with various forms of practice, finding one that will work for you is quite easy. Best of all, this gently leads us ultimately to a special place we often desire and want- greater understanding and acceptance of life's mysteries.

So, let's briefly explore the subject for the sole purpose of learning how to reap many beneficial rewards available through meditation. Besides, it is true, the best things in life are free. So let us begin to clear our minds of useless, wayward abstract thoughts having no justification to control or dictate our life's direction.

We will find meditation allows you in the purest sense, to create your own life's experiences. (More discussion about that possibility a bit later). For now, consider that during meditation you can replace, and clear out unwanted thoughts with life affirming versions gaining- a true, lasting peace of mind, body and soul. Meditation is your gateway offering all that and more...you can even create some magic in your life through this simple process!

As you may have heard or if you are already a dedicated practitioner, individuals report profound psychological, physical and spiritual well-being as they practice meditation daily. What then is meditation really all about? For beginners, how can one start? And how far can I go with sincere dedication? In this article we are going to examine a few areas- some historical background, benefits, science of the mind and advanced possibilities.

This book introduces you to certain meditation techniques that can take you to the epic journey of self-awareness. Whether you are a beginner or have been meditating for several months or years, this guide will take your experience, and your mindfulness practice, to the whole new level.

The author has shared his personal experiences on the journey of Awakening along with the benefits of meditation in your emotional well-being, physical health and your spiritual self in this insightful guide. The wisdom of meditation in the Middle Ages and the modern world and the myths keeping you from practicing meditation are also explained in the guide.

This book will guide you on how to live an easier, happier and fun-filled life by just meditating for 2 minutes a day. Awaken your mind, body and soul and improve your lifestyle quality and others around you.

Chapter 1: The History of Meditation

History and Importance of Meditation

The aim of meditation spans across different theologies, beliefs, and cultures. One can do it without being loaded with theological assumptions. For example, you don't need to be a Buddhist to practice mindfulness, an integral practice of meditation. You don't need to come from a specific country or a race in order to make meditation a part of your daily life.

In a broad sense, it's meant to cover everything from a deep psychological wound, to the faintest disturbances in one's everyday life. Where Buddhists view meditation as a means to ease life's suffering, Christianity's view argues that life is meant to be lived in love and that our main goal is to provide calm to a restless heart.

In a more secular take, detachment from the world offers a way for us to address the causes of our restlessness, suffering, and uneasiness. It acts as an alert system that focuses our attention and tells us that something is wrong. It becomes a way for us to perform self-awareness and pinpoint the source of our displeasure and fatigue. It is a practice aimed at caring for yourself and knowing yourself better through emptying the mind and attaining relaxation and inner peace.

According to many archeologists, meditation pre-dates written records. It could be easily envisioning a person entering an altered state of consciousness by simply gazing into the mind-stilling flicker of fire while thinking no thoughts. The earliest documented record of meditation comes from India in their Hindu scriptures called tantras.

These records date back over 5,000 years coming from the Indus valley and were combined with what is referred to today as yoga. Along with expanding trade, cultural exchange was also carried westward and meditation practice was soon embedded in eastern thought and spiritual practices.

With the advent of Buddha around 500 AD, many diverse cultures began to develop their own interpretations and specialized meditative techniques. Some techniques still in use to this day are said to deliver incredible mind-over-matter powers and supernormal skills that transform the practitioner.

Today, these are devout individuals and are not necessarily monks living in some remote mountain monastery. They are everyday people like you and I. Of course advancing through time, the long history of meditation is no longer only attributed to the Hindus and Buddhists. Not to be left out, Christianity, Islam and

Judaism also participate in the perpetuation of meditation each with its own take on the practice.

However, historically these religious faiths do not dominate in their teachings and practice a culture of meditation as compared to the Asian traditions. Meditation finds its place here in our Western culture in the early 1960s and into the '70s. This was a time when much of our culture was being tested, demanding to be redefined.

Meditation found fertile ground in which to flourish and expand. Some could say it was the "hippie" revolution which was inspired to embrace acceptance of foreign ideas, but only those that possessed real substantive value. It was not long after that when the Western medical and scientific community began to conduct research and studies on meditation. And what did most studies if not all, to varying degrees find?

You guessed it- significant health benefits. One of the most important aspects of meditation is how it releases stress from our bodies. This is achieved by bridging the gap between our conscious and un-conscious selves, situations or non-justified thoughts that permit stress to become less significant and actually lose its power. Through meditation, it does not take long before you feel more peaceful and relaxed about everything.

What happened to cause this nearly miraculous change? Studies have proven that meditation raises serotonin levels, which directly affect our behavior and emotional temperament. Conversely, low levels of serotonin lead to depression, headaches and even insomnia. All these are symptoms associated with stress.

Today, our western civilization with all our "advanced" knowledge has re-affirmed the ancient knowledge and understanding of meditation's therapeutic power to help alleviate mental and physical ailments. And this was just the infancy of discovery or shall we say re-discovery of unlimited powers available inside each of us.

Today, mediation without question is a universally medically accepted form of holistic healing used worldwide. Meditation could be summed up as a natural mechanism within each of us that enables the spirit within, the higher, true self to bridge the communication gap into our physical aspects, thus grounding us in unconditional love.

Where Meditation Comes From

When you think of meditation, do you envision an Asian monk or yogi in a loincloth or robe, sitting cross-legged in deep concentration? Well, meditation was definitely refined in the temples, caves, and monasteries of the East and Near East and fortunately for you and me, it has made its way West over the past 100 years or so. But meditation also appears, though less conspicuously and in slightly different form, in the Judeo-Christian tradition.

Did you know, for example, that many of the biblical prophets meditated? Or that Jesus engaged in some form of meditation when he retreated to the desert for 40 days?

Meditation dates back to our earliest ancestors, who gazed in wonder at the night sky, crouched in bushes for hours waiting for game, or sat in reverie beside communal fires. Because meditation involves a shift from thinking and doing to just being, our forebears had a headstart on you and me. After all, their lives were simpler, their thinking more rudimentary, and their connection to nature and the sacred far stronger.

Although you can certainly practice meditation without knowing where it comes from, tracing its development grounds it in a historical and spiritual context. So, join me for a brief overview of meditation's evolution as a sacred practice in various parts of the world.

The Indian Connection

You can find meditation's deepest roots in India, where sadhus (wandering holy men and women) and yogis have cultivated the practice in one form or another for more than 5,000 years. Attribute it to the climate, which slows the pace of life, or to the monsoon, which forces people to spend more time indoors, or just to the unbroken line of meditators over the ages. Whatever the reasons, India provided the fertile soil in which the meditative arts flourished and from which they spread both east and west.

The earliest Indian scriptures, the Vedas, don't even have a word for meditation, but the Vedic priests performed elaborate rites and chants to the gods that required tremendous concentration. Eventually, these practices evolved into a form of prayerful meditation that combined the use of breath control and devotional focus on the Divine. (See Chapter 1 for more on focus.)

The deeper they delved, the more these priests realized the worshipper and the object of worship, the individual being and the divine being itself, are one and the same. This was a profound insight that continued to inspire and instruct spiritual seekers through the ages.

From the garden of Vedic and post-Vedic spirituality sprouted three of India's best-known meditative traditions yoga, Buddhism, and tantra which I cover in the following sections.

Classical yoga: The path of blissful union

When you think of yoga, do you picture people twisting and stretching their bodies into challenging poses? Even if you practice hatha yoga yourself, what you may not know is that such "poses" are just one component of the traditional path of classical yoga, which includes breath control and meditation.

The practitioner of classical yoga aims to withdraw from the material world, which is considered illusory, and merge with the formless but ultimate reality of consciousness. After preparing the body with asanas (the familiar hatha yoga poses), cultivating refined energy states through various breathing practices, and excluding all external distractions.

The yogi focuses on an intermediate object, such as a mantra (repetition of a meaningful word or phrase) or a sacred symbol, and then on consciousness itself. Finally, the yogi arrives at a state known as samadhi, where all traces of separation dissolve and the yogi blissfully unites with consciousness.

Compiled and codified by Patanjali (a sage of the second century A.D.), the philosophy and practices of classical yoga gave rise to numerous and, at times, competing schools over the centuries. Most of the yogis and swamis who have taught in the West trace their lineage to classical yoga.

Early Buddhism: The roots of mindfulness meditation

The historical Buddha was a Hindu prince who, according to the traditional account, renounced his luxurious life to find answers to the mystery of suffering, old age, and death. After practicing asceticism and yoga for many years, he decided that rejecting the world and mortifying the flesh would not lead to the understanding he sought.

Instead, he sat down under a tree and began looking deeply into his own mind. After seven days and nights of intensive meditation, he woke up to the nature of existence, hence the name Buddha, or "the awakened one."

The Buddha taught that we suffer because we cling to the false belief that (a) things are permanent and can be relied upon for happiness and (b) we have an abiding self that exists independently of other beings and makes us who we are. Instead, he taught that everything changes constantly — our minds, our emotions, our sense of self, and the circumstances and objects in the external world.

To be free from suffering, he counseled, we must liberate ourselves from ignorance and eliminate fear, anger, greed, jealousy, and other negative mind- states. The approach he prescribed involves both practices for working with the mind and guidelines for living in the world in a virtuous and spiritual way.

Meditation lies at the heart of the historical Buddha's approach. The practice of meditation he taught, known as mindfulness, involves wakeful attention to our experience from moment to moment.

Here are the four traditional foundations of mindfulness:

- ✓ Awareness of the body
- ✓ Awareness of feelings
- ✓ Awareness of thoughts and mind-states
- ✓ Awareness of the laws of experience (the relationships between what we think and what we experience)

Departing from the other teachers of his day, who generally recommended withdrawing from the world to seek ecstatic union with the Divine, the Buddha taught the importance of gaining direct insight into the nature of existence and into how the mind creates suffering. He likened himself to a physician who offers medicine to heal wounds, rather than a philosopher who provides abstract answers to metaphysical questions.

Indian tantra: Finding the sacred in the world of the senses

Many Westerners associate the word tantra with traditional sexual practices that have been adapted to appeal to a popular audience. However, tantra developed in the early centuries A.D. as a major form of Indian spiritual practice and thought. Believing that absolute reality and the relative world of the senses are inseparable, tantrikas (practitioners of tantra) use the senses, including the practice of ritual sex as gateways to spiritual realization.

Needless to say, such an approach has its pitfalls; whereas yoga and Buddhism can veer toward life-denial, tantra can be confused with sensual indulgence.

Tantric meditation frequently involves practices for awakening the kundalini shakti, believed to be a powerful energy associated with the divine feminine that resides at the base of the spine. Once stimulated, the shakti rises through an energetic channel located in the spine and activates and opens each of the seven energy centers, or chakras, in its path. These centers, which vibrate at different frequencies and are associated with different physical and psychological functions, are located at the perineum, the genitals, the solar plexus, the heart, the throat, the forehead, and the crown of the head, respectively.

To the Roof of the World — and Beyond

Before it left India for good at the end of the first millennium A.D., Buddhism went through significant changes. The early teachings developed into what we now call Theravada — the dominant approach in Sri Lanka and Southeast Asia, emphasizing a progressive path to liberation largely limited to monks and nuns.

At the same time, another major current emerged that preached the ideal of the bodhisattva, the person who dedicates his or her life to liberating others. Known as the Mahayana ("the great vehicle"), this second major branch of Buddhism was more egalitarian and offered the possibility of enlightenment to everyone, whether lay or monastic.

From India, wandering monks and scholars transported Mahayana Buddhism over the Himalayas (the "roof of the world") to China and Tibet. There it min- gled with indigenous spiritual teachings, set down roots, and evolved into a number of different traditions and schools, most notably Ch'an (Zen in Japanese) and Vajrayana Buddhism, which took the practice of meditation to new heights

Vajrayana Buddhism: The way of transformation

Like China (where Buddhism encountered Taoism), Tibet had its indigenous religion, called Bonpo, which included magical practices designed to appease the local spirits and deities. When the great Indian master Padmasambhava brought Buddhism from India to Tibet in the seventh century A.D., he first had to conquer the hostile spirits that resisted his efforts. Ultimately, these spirits were incorporated into Tibetan Buddhism as protectors and allies in an elaborate pantheon that included various Buddhas and dakinis (awakened women).

Tibetan Buddhists believed the historical Buddha taught simultaneously at different levels, depending on the needs and abilities of his disciples. The most advanced teachings, they said, were kept secret for centuries and ultimately conveyed to Tibet as the Vajrayana ("the diamond way"). In addition to traditional mindfulness meditation, this approach incorporated elements of Indian tantra and involved powerful practices for working with energy.

Instead of eliminating negative emotions and mind-states like anger, greed, and fear, as traditional Buddhism recommends, the Vajrayana teaches practitioners how to transform negativity directly into wisdom and compassion.

Meditation in Tibetan Buddhism also employs visualization — the active use of the imagination to invoke potent spiritual forces that fuel the process of spiritual realization.

From the Middle East to the Rest of the West

Although meditation in the Judeo-Christian and Islamic traditions had its own independent development, meditators in the Middle East may have been influenced by the practices of their counterparts in India and Southeast Asia

Historians do have evidence traders and pilgrims traveled between the two regions constantly, and Buddhist monks appeared in Rome in early Christian times! There's even the rumor, buoyed by some interesting historical coincidences, that Jesus may have learned how to meditate in India.

While Indian meditators — following the ancient insight that atman equals Brahman ("I and the ground of being are one"), turned their attention progressively inward, seeking the sacred in the depths of their own being, Western thinkers and theologians pointed to a God who purportedly exists outside the individual. At the same time, mystics in the West wrestled with the paradox that God is both inside and outside, personal and transcendent.

Meditation in the Western religions usually takes the form of prayer — that is, direct communion with God. But the meditative prayer of the monks and mystics differs from ordinary prayer, which often includes complaints and requests. Instead, meditative prayer approaches God with humility and devotion, contemplates His divine qualities, and invites His presence into the heart of the meditator. Ultimately, the goal is to surrender the individual self completely in union with the Divine.

Christian meditation: Practicing contemplative prayer

The Christian equivalent of meditation, known as contemplative prayer, dates back to Jesus himself, who fasted and prayed in the desert for 40 days and nights. In contemplation, says Father Thomas Keating, whose "centering prayer" has helped revitalize interest in Christian meditation, you open your awareness and your heart to God, the ultimate mystery, who dwells in the depths of your being, beyond the reach of the mind.

After the time of Jesus, the first great Christian meditators were the desert fathers of Egypt and Palestine in the third and fourth centuries, who lived largely in solitude and cultivated awareness of the Divine presence through constant repetition of a sacred phrase. Their direct descendants, the monks, nuns, and mystics of medieval Europe, developed the contemplative practice of repeating and ruminating over a scriptural passage (not to be confused with thinking about or analyzing it!) until its deeper significance revealed itself to the mind. Both of these practices, explains Father Keating, hark back to Jesus's admonition, "When you pray, go into your closet, your innermost being, and bolt the door."

In the Eastern Orthodox Church of Greece and Eastern Europe, monks have long engaged in a similar practice combining prostrations (full-body bows) with the repetition of the Jesus prayer ("Lord Jesus Christ have mercy on me, a sinner") until all practices drop away to reveal a deep interior silence filled with love and bliss.

In recent years, many Christian ministers and monastics have been influenced by the Hindu and Buddhist teachers who have appeared in the West in increasing numbers.

In response, some have adapted Eastern practices to the needs of Christian audiences. Others, like Father Keating, have delved into their own contemplative roots and resuscitated practices that had become dusty with disuse.

Meditation in Judaism: Drawing closer to God

According to Rami Shapiro, rabbi of Temple Beth Or in Miami, Florida, and author of Wisdom of the Jewish Sages, mystical interpreters of the Bible have found evidence of meditation dating back to Abraham, the founder of Judaism.

The Old Testament prophets apparently entered into altered states of con- sciousness through fasting and ascetic practices, and mystics in the first few centuries A.D. meditated on a vision of the prophet Ezekiel.

But the first formal Jewish meditation, says Shapiro, centered on the Hebrew alphabet, which was considered the divine language through which God created the world. "If you could see into the alphabet," explains Shapiro, "you could see into the source of creation and thereby become one with the creator Himself."

Like practitioners in all the God-centered religions, Jewish meditators have traditionally used sacred phrases or verses from scripture as mantras to bring them closer to God. As one great Hasidic master used to say of the phrase r'bono shel olam ("master of the universe"), if you just repeat it continuously, you will achieve union with God.

And it is precisely this union that Jewish meditation intends to induce. Like Christianity, Judaism has been inspired by Eastern influences in recent years to revive its own meditative traditions. Rabbis like Shapiro (who practices Zen meditation) and David Cooper (who trained in Buddhist mindfulness meditation) are creating a Jewish meditative renaissance by forging a new synthesis of ancient techniques from East and West.

Meditation among the Sufis: Surrendering to the Divine with every breath. Since the time of the prophet Mohammed in the seventh century A.D., Sufis have worn the garments of Islam. But, according to the American-born Sufi teacher Shabda Kahn, their roots go back much farther, beyond Mohammed or Buddha or other famous teachers, to the first awakened person.

Sufisclaim to be a fellowship of mystical seekers whose sole purpose is to realize the Divine in their own hearts. The forms of Sufism have varied from century to century and teacher to teacher and from one geographical location to another, but the basic teaching is the same:

There is nothing but God. Meditation in Sufism generally takes the form of chanting a sacred phrase, either silently or out loud, while breathing deeply and rhythmically — a practice known as zikr, "remembrance of the Divine." Kahn explains that Sufis retranslate the Biblical beatitude

"Blessed are the poor in spirit" to "Blessed are those who have a refined breath."

When the Sufi has cultivated and refined the breath, he or she can use it as a method for surrendering to the divine presence in each moment with every breath.

The Americanization of Meditation

If you harken back to the counterculture of the 1960s and 1970s to find the first seeds of meditation on American soil, you may be surprised to discover that the roots go far deeper. Some of the earliest settlers transplanted Eastern ideas when they fled to the colonies, seeking freedom for their particular brand of Christianity. And many of the framers of the Declaration of Independence and the U.S. Constitution — men like Thomas Jefferson and Benjamin Franklin — belonged to secret fraternities informed by the mystical teachings of Sufism and Judaism.

Transcendentalism and Theosophy (1840–1900)

The first major influx of Eastern teachings began in the 1840s and 1850s, when Transcendentalists like Emerson and Thoreau read Hindu scriptures in English translations of German adaptations from the Sanskrit! While Thoreau, whose ideas on civil disobedience were influenced by Eastern philosophy, withdrew to Walden Pond to meditate in nature, his good friend Emerson was blending German idealism, Yankee optimism, and Indian spirituality to formulate his version of the Transcendentalist credo. In the process, he transformed the Hindu Brahman (the divine ground of being) into a more universal concept he called the Oversoul.

Later in the century, the Theosophists members of a largely Western move- ment, led by the Russian-born Madame Blavatsky, who adapted and popularized Indian spiritual thought, made Hindu meditation texts available to the ordinary reader, and followers of the New Thought movement practiced guided visualizations and mantra meditations adapted from Eastern sources.

But the landmark meditation event of the 19th century turned out to be the World Parliament of Religions, an international gathering of religious leaders and teachers held in Chicago in 1893. For the first time, Asian masters presented their teachings directly to Westerners on American soil. Following the conference, several of the masters (including the Indian sage Swami Vivekananda and the Japanese Zen teacher Soyen Shaku) toured the United States lecturing to interested audiences.

Yoga and Zen prepare the soil (1900–1960)

In the decades following the World Parliament, the Zen monk Nyogen Senzaki continued Soyen Shaku's work of sowing the seeds of meditation in the New World, and Swami Paramananda, a disciple of Swami Vivekananda, established centers where curious Americans could practice meditation and hear sophisticated Indian spiritual teachings. (The Vedanta Society, which grew up around the work of swamis Vivekananda and Paramananda and their disciples, continues to flourish in the United States and Europe.)

In the 1920s, the Indian yogi Paramahansa Yogananda settled in the United States, and his work gradually blossomed into the Self-Realization Fellowship, which today boasts followers throughout the Western world.

Perhaps the best-known spiritual teacher to arrive during this period was J. Krishnamurti, who settled in Southern California in the 1940s and attracted the English writers Aldous Huxley and Christopher Isherwood. Although Krishnamurti (who was groomed from childhood to be a world teacher by the Theosophists) shunned formal meditation and religious dogma in favor of dialogue and self-inquiry, Huxley and Isherwood helped to popularize the great Hindu scriptures.

By the 1950s, Zen began to significantly influence the American counterculture. While the poet Gary Snyder (who later won the Pulitzer Prize for his book Turtle Island) was off studying Zen in Japan, his friend and Beat colleague Jack Kerouac wrote novels that popularized Buddhist concepts such as dharma, karma, and satori. Also in the '50s, the great Japanese scholar D.

T. Suzuki began teaching Zen at Columbia University in New York City, where his audiences included the young Thomas Merton, novelist J. D. Salinger, composer John Cage, and psychoanalysts Erich Fromm and Karen Horney.

About the same time, the books of former Episcopalian priest and Zen afi- cionado Alan Watts including The Way of Zen and Psychotherapy East and West became popular sellers.

Meditation reaches Main Street (1960 to the present)

In the 1960s, a unique cluster of events set the stage for the mainstreaming of meditation. Many Baby Boomers, who were now reaching young adulthood, began experimenting with altered states of consciousness by using so-called mind-expanding drugs like marijuana and LSD. At the same time, the war in Vietnam prompted a national backlash among a sizable segment of the population and helped forge a counterculture opposed in many ways to the status quo.

Popular music fueled the fires of discontent and touted the benefits of "tuning in, turning on, and dropping out" — words that in another time, place, and context might have referred to renouncing the world in favor of the monastic life. And political unrest in Asia (including shock waves from Vietnam and the Chinese takeover of Tibet) combined with the spirit of the times to bring a new wave of spiritual teachers to the New World.

From the standpoint of meditation, perhaps the landmark event of this era was the conversion of the Beatles to the practice of Transcendental Meditation (TM), which prompted thousands of their young fans to begin meditating, too. (Over the years, the TM movement has taught millions of Westerners how to meditate and has pioneered research revealing the mind-body benefits of meditation.)

As psychedelics lost their luster, more and more people who had looked to drugs to provide meditative experiences like peace and insight turned to the real thing — and some even took refuge in the yoga communities and Zen centers constructed by their newfound teachers.

Since the 1970s, a new generation, with the savvy to translate the teachings for their brothers and sisters, has emerged in the West as sanctioned teachers of Eastern spiritual disciplines. As Alan Watts anticipated (in his book Psychotherapy East and West), the field of psychotherapy has been particularly open to Eastern influences — perhaps because psychotherapy, like meditation, purports to offer a solution for suffering. As a result, American spiritual teachers often couch their messages in language that appeals to proponents of "personal growth."

At the same time, scientific researchers like Herbert Benson, Jon Kabat-Zinn, and Dean Ornish have pioneered the mainstreaming of meditation (see the sidebar "Promoting the benefits of meditation" in Chapter 2), and books on meditation and related topics regularly appear on the New York Times bestseller list. In one six-month period recently, Time magazine ran a cover story on the growing popularity of Buddhism, and Newsweek ran covers featuring the faces of Ornish and best-selling author and meditation expert Deepak Chopra. Without doubt, meditation has emerged as a mainstream American practice!

Chapter 2: Benefits of Meditation for the Body, Mind, and Soul

Much has been said about the many benefits of meditation. However, different people have different experiences with it. Others may feel it gives them a sense of smooth calm and they can let go of emotional burdens. Others may also feel like meditation is making them work hard to train their mind and thus take control of certain situations. Still, the benefits grossly outweigh the cons, and meditation is the perfect technique to give you an overall sense of well-being.

You don't have to join some cult or get baptized or bar mitzvahed to enjoy the benefits of meditation. And you don't have to check out of your everyday life and run off to a monastery in the Himalayas. You simply need to practice your meditation regularly without trying to get anywhere or achieve anything. Like interest in a money-market account, the benefits just accrue by themselves.

To awaken to the present moment

When you rush breathlessly from one moment to the next, anticipating another problem or hungering for another pleasure, you miss the beauty and immediacy of the present, which is constantly unfolding before your eyes.

Meditation teaches you to slow down and take each moment as it comes, the sounds of traffic, the smell of new clothes, the laughter of children, the worried look on an old woman's face, the coming and going of your breath. In fact, as the meditative traditions remind us, only the present moment exists anyway, the past is just a memory and the future a fantasy, projected on the movie screen of the mind right now.

To make friends with yourself

When you're constantly struggling to live up to images and expectations (your own or someone else's) or racing to reinvent yourself to survive in a competitive environment, you rarely have the opportunity or the motivation to get to know yourself just the way you are.

Self-doubt and self-hatred may appear to fuel the fires of self-improvement, but they're painful and besides, they contribute to other negative mind-states, such as fear, anger, depression, and alienation, and prevent you from living up to your full potential.

When you meditate, you learn to welcome every experience and facet of your being without judgment or denial. In the process, you begin to treat yourself as you would a close friend, accepting (and even loving) the whole package, the apparent weaknesses and shortcomings as well as the positive qualities and strengths.

To connect more deeply with others

As you awaken to the present moment and open your heart and mind to your own experience, you naturally extend this quality of awareness and presence to your relationships with family and friends. If you're like the rest of us, you tend to project your own desires and expectations onto the people close to you, which acts as a barrier to real communication. But when you start to accept others the way they are, a skill you can cultivate through the practice of meditation — you open up the channels for a deeper love and intimacy to flow between you.

To relax the body and calm the mind

As contemporary health researchers have discovered and traditional texts agree mind and body are inseparable, and an agitated mind inevitably produces a stressed-out body. As the mind settles, relaxes, and opens during meditation, so does the body and the longer you meditate (measured both in minutes logged each day and in days and weeks of regular practice), the more this peace and relaxation ripples out to every area of your life, including your health.

To lighten up

Perhaps you've noticed that nonstop thinking and worrying generate a kind of inner claustrophobia fears feed on one another, problems get magnified exponentially, and the next thing you know, you're feeling overwhelmed and panicked. Meditation encourages an inner mental spaciousness in which difficulties and concerns no longer seem so threatening and constructive solutions can naturally arise. It also offers a certain detachment that allows for greater objectivity, perspective, and, yes, humor. That mysterious word enlightenment actually refers to the supreme "lightening up!"

To enjoy more happiness

Research reveals the daily practice of doing meditation for just a few months actually makes people happier, as measured not only by their subjective reports, but also by brain-mapping technology. In fact, meditation is apparently the only thing that can permanently change your emotional set point your basic level of relative happiness that scientists say stays the same throughout your life, no matter what you experience.

If you want lasting happiness, leading-edge science and spiritual wisdom have the same advice to offer: Forget about winning the lottery or landing the perfect job — and begin meditating instead!

To experience focus and flow

When you're so fully involved in an activity that all sense of self-consciousness, separation, and distraction dissolves, you've entered what psychologist

No doubt you've experienced moments like these creating a work of art, playing a sport, working in the garden, making love. Athletes call it "the zone." Through meditation, you can discover how to give the same focused attention to and derive the same enjoyment from every activity.

To feel more centered, grounded, and balanced

To counter the escalating insecurity of life in rapidly changing times, meditation offers an inner groundedness and balance that external circumstances can't destroy. When you practice coming home again and again to your body, your breath, your sensations, your feelings you eventually grow to realize you're always home, no matter where you go. And when you make friends with yourself, embracing the dark and the light, the weak and the strong you no longer get thrown off-center by the "slings and arrows" of life.

To enhance your performance at work and at play

Studies have shown basic meditation practice alone can enhance perceptual clarity, creativity, self-actualization, and many of the other factors that contribute to superior performance. In addition, specific meditations have been devised to enhance performance in a variety of activities, from sports to schoolwork.

To increase appreciation, gratitude, and love

As you begin to open to your experience without judgment or aversion, your heart gradually opens as well to yourself and others. You can practice specific meditations for cultivating appreciation, gratitude, and love. Or you may find, as so many meditators have before you, that these qualities arise naturally when you can gaze at the world with fresh eyes, free from the usual projections and expectations.

To align with a deeper sense of purpose

When you practice making the shift from doing and thinking to being, you discover how to align yourself with a deeper current of meaning and belonging. You may get in touch with personal feelings and aspirations that have long remained hidden from your conscious awareness. Or you may connect with a more universal source of purpose and direction some people call the higher self or inner guidance.

To awaken to a spiritual dimension of being

As your meditation gradually opens you to the subtlety and richness of each fleeting but irreplaceable moment, you may naturally begin to see through the veil of appearances to the sacred reality at the heart of things and you eventually may come to realize (and this one could take lifetimes!) the very same sacred reality is actually who you are in your own heart of hearts.

This deep insight what the sages and masters call "waking up from the illusion of separation" cuts through and ultimately eliminates loneliness and alienation and opens you to the beauty of the human condition.

Improved focus

In terms of creative work, meditation helps with productivity. Training the brain through meditation techniques can be likened to training muscles – you constantly work to make them stronger. Intensive meditation trains you to keep your focus on a task and sustain it, despite the most boring of tasks. This provides you more time to do other things you need or want to do.

Uplift mood

If you are the type to stress over the little things, then meditation can help in detaching yourself from the outer world and not allowing you to sweat the small stuff. It trains your mind to stop considering every small task as an issue that is critical or immense in nature. Instead of spending all your time worrying, you can train yourself to fully participate in the now and live in the present. It allows you to react in the most efficient way possible, so you can lessen the stress in your daily life. With this, you will eventually learn to see the bigger picture.

Better health

Meditation alleviates nervousness and it helps in reducing stress. Stress-related symptoms such as irritable bowel syndrome, fibromyalgia, or post-traumatic stress disorder can significantly improve as well. Since meditation helps in promoting better sleep and quality rest, it can lead to lowered blood pressure levels, decreased chance of developing depression and anxiety, and it inhibits the release of inflammation-inducing chemicals called cytokines. It also reduces the stress hormone called cortisol normally associated with both physical and mental stress.

For people who are used to high-pressure work or life environment, habitual meditation can help control anxiety-related mental health issues such as social anxiety, obsessive-compulsive behaviors and phobias among others.

Self-awareness

When one is self-aware, this can lead to an improved self-image and a considerable boost in self-esteem. This is where one can benefit from meditation. Studies show those who meditate develop changes in the areas of the brain related to positive thinking and optimism. This is because when one is self-aware, you have a better understanding of yourself, which can help you grow into your best self.

The great thing about meditation is it goes beyond any of your religious beliefs, philosophy, and values. Rather, it finds direct access to your heart and soul. Meditation is something that can easily be done by anyone. After all, what is the purpose of life if you're not there to enjoy it?

Once inner peace of mind takes over you, you will start to find joy and fun in everything you do. Meditation can be likened to a stream tha tis ever shifting and changing as it passes smoothly through a valley. When you practice it, you can develop the ability to change its course in accordance to how you need to respond and react to your surroundings and to the environment around you.

There is no such thing as perfect meditation. But the important thing is you meditate consistently. You may find your thoughts wandering or you may even forget to follow your breathing, and that's ok.

Other benefits of meditation include, but are not limited to: decreased blood pressure, lesser perspiration, improved quality of blood circulation, slower heart rate and respiratory rate, lower blood cortisol level, more feelings of well-being and less stress as well as less anxiety, and deeper and more meaningful relaxation.

Consistent meditation often yields these benefits as the immune system in humans improves drastically with consistency of meditation practice.

However, it's worth noting that the goal is not to achieve benefits, but simply to be present. The liberated or the enlightened practitioner of meditation no longer has the need to follow desires or to cling to experiences and strong internal emotions. Instead, he just maintains a calm and peaceful, sound mind.

Chapter 3: The Different Concepts of Meditation

The "deep rest" achieved through the practice of meditation can eliminate stress, confusion, and uncertainty and allow the individual to make better decisions through clearer and more focused thinking. In addition, in many cases, meditation has been proven to improve self-esteem in individuals with low self-confidence.

The concepts of meditation are almost identical to those of yoga, as their aims a very similar. Both sects of self-healing depend on the participant freeing themselves of any outside distraction or influence and focusing on the development of their mind/body disconnection and self-improvement.

While the practice of Yoga is more of a physical route to such a separation, meditation uses the mind (or lack thereof in some cases) to achieve Dharma. The following concepts will look similar to those of yoga, but with a few key changes in approach and goal.

Karma

This concept refers to any type of physical or mental action. In addition, this concept deals with the consequences of each action. An easy way to understand this concept lies in the Biblical law of "an eye for an eye." You must expect to eventually receive any action you force onto another person in your future life.

There are actually three types of karma. The first is all acts performed in all lives (reincarnation). The second is the acts of you current life. The third type of karma is the acts you are performing right now.

Swadharma

Swadhara is the obligation that a spirit has to follow dharma. Where dharma regards the rules and guidelines, swadhara pertains to the need for a spirit to follow those rules. This concept is much related to altruistic principles and instinctive feelings such as maternal and fraternal.

According to the teachings of Meditation, every individual spirit will have a different level of swadhara. This level will determine their dharma and can be raised through meditation or reduced through lack thereof.

Dharma

This concept deals with the correct way to live your life and receive good karma. This concept not only concerns itself with physical and mental acts against other spirits, but also with the ability of the practitioner to achieve enlightenment and a union with the supreme being. This may sound familiar to followers of all types of religion that claim that good deeds alone are not enough to achieve immortality.

Manah

This concept is the Sanskrit word for your mind. However, the manah is not the entire mind. The manah is the portion of the mind that receives sensory signals from other portions of the body. This is not only the scientific concept of sensory perception, but the metaphysical ability for the mind to receive signals from the spirit.

Buddhi

The Sanskrit term for intelligence. This concept is the conscious ability to be able to understand the concepts taught to you. It also concerns itself with the ability to think through situations and to use reason when making important decisions. Your overall intelligence is referred to as your buddhi.

Samskara

This concept is literally translated as your memories. Basically, every action you perform (whether good or bad) creates an impression stored in your mind. Negative impressions must be cleansed in order to obtain immortality. In addition to being a moral protection device, this concept also deals with maternal and fraternal instincts.

Vasana

When your mind stores impressions of actions, or memories (samskara), they are typically grouped together based on similarities between them. These groups are referred to as vasana. These bundles are unconscious and must be restored through deep focus and meditation.

These bundles are active even if they are held in the unconscious. For example, you may be triggered to perform another "happy" bundle of actions because they left positive impressions in the past. In addition to acting as constantly referenced emotions, these bundles are what govern the development of experience and maturity.

Kriya

This concept refers to the actual practice or exercise of the techniques found in Yoga. It not only pertains to the actual correct physical motions involved, but also the correction of incorrect technique and the skill involved in performing each movement.

These motions are intended to have a purifying effect on the body in small amounts. Performing these motions will result in higher levels of metaphysical awareness and a heightened sense of purpose or being.

Viveka

This concept is directly related to the ability to realize the difference between reality and the fantasy or unrealistic portion of life. Not only does it involve knowing the difference between realism and the opposite, but also the difference between the temporary aspects of life and the permanent aspects of the current and after life.

When employing this concept, the practitioner must remember to constantly review what is real and what is fake and employ proper reactions based on their discoveries.

Vairagya

Vairagya concerns itself with the disinterest in anything of the current life. This concept requires the participant to distance himself from anything they enjoy in their mortal life in order to better prepare for the after life. This includes the indifference of possessions, enjoyed feelings and the enjoyment of any emotional action or response.

Sannyasa

This is the concept that attempts to sum up all other concepts that contribute to a well led life. It involves adherence to all other concepts and is the eventual pursuit of perfection in all aspects of life to attain a truly healthy and perfect afterlife.

Focused Attention Meditation

In this type of meditation, you will need to fix your focus on a particular object for the duration of the whole session. This object may be a mantra, a part of your body, a breathing technique, or a visualization of an external object. Here are several focus points you may use:

- ✓ A mantra – Repetition of a word, phrase, or sound over and over

- ✓ Visualization – Picturing a place you may or may not have been to, or simply focusing on a goal

- ✓ A body part – Placing focus on a particular area of your body

- ✓ Candle – Staring intently at a flame in order to focus the mind

- ✓ Mala beads – Counting the beads on a mala

- ✓ A sound – Focusing on your hearing and listening to the sound of a chime or a gong

The main focus on this type of meditation is simply to keep your attention focused on a particular thing and nothing else. In doing so, you will only keep focused on that particular flame from the candle, or to the sound of the gong, and your mind would just engage in that practice. Like everything else, this type of meditation improves with practice, and soon you will find the lapses and distractions will eventually lessen until they completely fade away.

There is a subset of this type of focused attention meditation technique, and it is called Samatha meditation. This is when one pays close attention to the sensations of inhalation and exhalation without the need to force your attention on it. The goal is simply to observe the natural breathing process in a gentle manner. Samatha meditation can also allow you to focus on other body parts such as the rising and falling of your chest as you breathe, your nostrils as the flow of air enters and exits your nose, the upper lip and the air that is moving across it, and the expansion and contraction of the diaphragm.

Effortless patience

As the name suggests, you don't need to exercise too much effort or though into meditation with this technique. Otherwise known as choice-less awareness" or "pure being," this goes against the traditional meditation method where you focus on a particular object or thought. You just allow your mind to wander off and find a sense of calm from it. This way, you can train your mind to develop a deeper sense of consciousness and inner silence.

Open Monitoring Meditation

This is another type of meditation where you need to be open and allow yourself to see all the parts of your experience without judging. Examples of this type of meditation include Vipassana, Mindfulness meditation, and Taoist meditation.

Zen or Zazen Meditation

From the Japanese word that means "seated meditation", Zen meditation is rooted in Chinese Buddhism that dates back to the 6th century. It is generally practiced by being seated on a cushion or a mat on the floor with the legs crossed. This is often referred to as half-lotus or lotus position. Zen meditation often helps in improving one's concentration and is highly favored among communities that regularly perform or advocate meditation.

You will need to keep your back straight, with mouth closed, and eyes lowered. There are two ways to perform the Zen meditation technique:

Breathing – This is where you need to place your focus on breathing through the nose, and counting the breath in your mind. Once you inhale, counting starts from 10 and goes back to 9,8, 7, and so on. If you find yourself getting lost or distracted, you can start counting from 10 again.

Sitting and remaining in the present moment – Just like effortless meditation, you don't really need to use any particular object. Instead, you just need to remain in the present and be as aware as you possibly can. Try not to exercise judgement on anything else in your outside environment and try to be present at all times.

Vipassana Meditation

This is another type of Buddhist meditation practice that was founded in the 6th century BC and comes from the Theravada Buddhism sect. Vipassana refers to "clear sighting" or "insight." To put it into practice, you only need to sit on the floor in a comfortable position, making sure your spine is erect. You may also use a chair, but you need to make sure that you back is not supported in any way.

With every moment, you will need to focus attention on your breathing. With every rise and fall of your abs, you will need to place your attention on this, along with the feeling of air going in and out through your nostrils. As you focus on this breathing technique, you will need to observe all other sensations you are feeling such as sounds and emotions. Just notice them and then go back to breathing. All other sensations and thoughts are considered background noise and need not be taken in as part of your breathing awareness.

The Vipassana meditation technique is a wonderful way to get to know how your mind works and discover your personality on a deeper level.

Mindfulness Meditation

Adapted from the typical Buddhist practices such as Vipassana, Mindfulness meditation is influenced by Vietnamese Zen Buddhism. Fast forward to the 1970s when it was made even more popular and mainstream by John Kabet-Zinn, who pioneered its use in various healthcare units and hospitals.

Mindfulness meditation can be practiced simply by placing focus on your current situation and moment, and thus accepting every sensation that comes along with it. Every thought and emotion that strikes in your mind should also be included without placing any judgement on it.

To perform this formally, you will need to sit on a chair or the floor on a cushion with an unsupported or straight back and closely focus on the movement of your breath. While breathing, take note and be aware of the breathing and your feelings. While you exhale, take notice. When you get distracted, get back to the technique as soon as you possibly can.

Background noise such as sounds, sensations, and thoughts will come and distract you, but once it happens, do not pay further notice to these things. Recognize them as distractions and focus back on your breathing. There is a difference between being inside the sensation or thought and being aware of it.

The great thing about mindfulness is you can practice it in your daily life. You can do it while you are walking, or when you're eating, or even talking to someone. All you need to do is to focus your attention on what you are doing in the present moment. Be aware of what the situation is arising around you. When you speak, pay attention to how you are speaking to them and listen to others with attention and patience if you are talking with them. When you walk, be aware of your movements. Feel how your feet touches the ground and pay attention to the sounds you are actually hearing.

Mindfulness meditation is probably the most recommended and easiest way to start meditating if you are just a beginner. Because of its simplicity, it is now mostly taught at hospitals and schools. The mindfulness movement as a whole is even practiced in societies nowadays to ensure good mental and physical health, as well as overall well-being.

The technique in itself is very easy to incorporate in your daily routine. As a start in your spiritual development, mindfulness meditation can evoke deeper transformation in your life. As you go along, you can then progress and make a move towards other meditation forms such as Vipassana, Zazen, or other techniques.

Metta Meditation

Also known as "loving kindness meditation," Metta refers to benevolence, good health, and kindness. It traces its origins back to Tibetan and Theravada lineages. This type of compassion meditation showcases the efficacy of meditative practices related to metta. It helps in developing positive emotions with compassion. A sense of loving feeling towards others, as well as feelings of competence about someone else's life, higher self-acceptance, and feel of the purpose of life sums up what metta meditation aims to do.

With your eyes closed, you will need to sit in a relaxed meditation posture. You will need to generate feelings of compassion and kindness. Develop these feelings of kindness towards yourself, before projecting them towards others. You may need to generate these feelings firstly on yourself, then to a good friend, any neutral person, towards a difficult friend, everyone else, and then finally to the rest of the world. The more you practice this technique, the more happiness you will feel.

Metta meditation is recommended for those who can sometimes be too hard on themselves or on others. It can help in the improvement of your relationships and is good for both selfless and self-centered people. It can also boost and enhance feelings of pleasure and satisfaction in life; therefore, it is a great tool to combat depression. Buddhist teachers often recommend this to help with anger issues, insomnia problems, or as an antidote to frequent nightmares.

Mantra Meditation

Mantra is a particular word or syllable which really has no specific meaning but is repeatedly said to focus your mind. There are meditation teachers who believe in the power of a mantra and how it is the only way to focus your mind regardless of the chosen word or phrase that becomes your mantra. Mantras are widely used in Buddhist traditions, Hindu traditions, as well as Sikhism, Jainism, and Taoism (Daoism). Mantra meditation is also known as Om meditation.

This technique is performed just like with any meditation types, where you sit, your eyes are closed and you have your back straight. Then you will need to repeat the mantra in your mind, again and again, for the rest of the session. You will also need to observe your breathing and coordinate with it. Sometimes, the mantra is whispered very softly and lightly and this helps to make the practitioners stay focused.

When you chant the mantra, it then creates vibes in which your mind can feel the awareness that is happening at a deeper level. During the period of meditation, the mantra then becomes indistinct and abstract, until you get back into a state of complete consciousness. As you constantly repeat the mantra, you get to completely disconnect yourself from all other distractions.

Mantra can help you in practicing meditation, and some of the most famous and commonly used mantras are the following: Om, Om namah shivaya, Rama, Yam, Ham, Om Mani Padme Hum. Practice saying these mantras for a specific period of time, usually for 108 or 1,008 times with the help of beads as your guide to keep counting. As you go deeper into chanting the mantra, you will eventually notice that mantra keeps humming in your mind all by itself. It may even vanish sometimes as you are enjoying the intense inner peace.

Mantra meditation is usually very easy to focus on doing as compared to breathing. This is because thoughts appear in words, which makes it altogether easier to perform than breathing. For those whose mind races with several thoughts and can easily get distracted, it is very useful and needs regular attention. You may find that as you meditate, you will lose your consciousness as you delve deeper in the mantra, eventually becoming very indistinct and abstract.

Practicing it for a specific of time, usually for 108 or 1,008 times, can be very taxing at first. Because of this, you may benefit from using beads to help you keep counting. Later on, the mantra may seem to keep on going even when you're not, humming in its own rhythm. Sometimes, it may even vanish, leaving one to enjoy the sense of inner calm and peace that comes with being very deep into meditation.

It is usually very easy to pair mantra meditation with breathing. For those whose mind is always a busy place for interjecting thoughts, repeating a mantra can help in keeping your focus and attention because the task of repeating the mantra needs constant and regular attention.

Yoga Meditation

Yoga is a very popular exercise that is now widely practiced the world over. Many claim to have reaped its numerous benefits, both physically, mentally, emotionally, or spiritually. Yoga simply refers to "union" and its tradition dates back to 1700 BC. It has been regarded as having the highest spiritual purification and self-awareness. The beginning of pre-classical yoga was developed by the Indus-Sarasvati civilization in Northern India. By the time classical yoga was organized by Patanjali's Yoga-Sutras, there was a systematic presentation of yoga that contained steps and stages towards attaining enlightenment.

Classic Yoga is divided int the following: Asanas (Physical postures), Niyamas (Rules of Conduct), Pranayama (Breathing exercises), Dharana, Pratyahara, Samadhi, Dhyana (Contemplative techniques. There are many different ways to practice yoga meditation techniques and here are several of them:

Third Eye Meditation – To perform this, focus on the spot in between your eyebrows. You will need to constantly put your focus on this point in order to silence your mind, resulting in making the silent gaps between your thoughts getting deeper and wider.

Chakra Meditation – In this type of meditation, you will need to focus on the "centers of your energy," otherwise known as the Chakras of your body. This is done by chanting a special mantra or doing several visualizations.

Kundalini Yoga – This complex form of yoga helps to awaken the "Kundalini Energy," which is located at the base of the spine. This technique is highly specialized and should only be done with the help of a qualified yogi because of the associated risks involved.

Gazing Meditation – As the name implies, you will need to fix your gaze on any external object with this type of mediation. It can be anything from a symbol, a candle, an image, or a person. You will be required to do this with your eyes wide open at first and then with your eyes closed. This will help you train both the visualization and concentration abilities of your mind. After closing the eyes, you need to keep the image of the object in your mind afterwards.

Nada Yoga – Also called sound meditation, you will need to start listening to external sounds in this technique. For example, you may choose to listen to any soothing and calming ambient music so that you will be able to focus all your attention on hearing and listening in order to quiet your mind. As time progresses, you will then begin to hear the internal sound of your own mind and body.

Kriya Yoga – This is a set of energizations, meditation and breathing all in one. It was taught by Paramhamsa Yogananda. It is most beneficial for those with a devotional temperament as one can use it to explore the spiritual parts of meditation.

Pranayama – This is not exactly meditation per se, but rather, a way to calm your mind and train it for meditation. The simplest and most common type of Pranayama is 4-4-4-4. With this, you will need to breathe in and out up to the count of 4, hold your breath for 4 seconds, then exhale the air for about another 4 seconds, and then finally hold still for the last 4 seconds. You will need to breathe through your nostrils and your stomach and abs absorb it. This breathing control helps in lifting your mood.

There are many different ways to practice yoga meditation, so much that there is bound to be one perfect fit or two for just about anyone. Find one that is most suitable to your personality and needs, and one you find very simple and easy to do. For example, music lovers may favor Nada yoga over anything else simply because it involves the use of music during meditation. If you have a more devotional personality, then Kriya yoga might be your yoga meditation technique of choice.

On the other hand, if you are the type to learn better with the help of a teacher, then either the Chakra or the Kundalini is your best bet. The easiest option may be the Third eye meditation because it yields better and faster results. You may also need to get more instructions to perform other types of yoga, and in addition, you can also try Pranayama if you are new to meditation in general.

Transcendental Meditation

Self-inquiry is the main core of Transcendental yoga, and this involves a deeper investigation to the nature of your true self. It is all about answering the complex question of "who am I?" and delves into self-awareness like no other meditation technique can. Popularized during the 20th century, several contemporary meditators employ this technique. It involves a very simple yet subtle practice. To know how it works, one must first understand a few basic abstract concepts. The central part of your world is your sense of "ego" to "I". It exists behind all your thoughts, emotions, memories, and perceptions. We also often confuse the "I" with our minds, bodies, our roles in the family and society as a whole, or our status and social standing. Go deep with the "who am I?" question, beyond any of the obvious role sor titles you have in life and delve deeper into your actual "I."

This technique is very effective and powerful, as it helps bring feelings of inner peace and freedom. However, it may be hard to follow if you do not have any experience with meditation whatsoever.

Chinese Meditation

The origin of Chinese meditation can be rooted back to Taoism or Daoism - the religion and philosophy which dates back to Lao Tzu. Tao Te Ching is the main text which came into existence during the 6th century BC. Some of the lineages and passages were also inspired from the Buddhist meditation from India, in the 8th century BC.

Transformation, generation, and circulation of inside energy are the main characteristics of this meditation technique. It helps to quiet the mind and the body, unify both the body and the spirit, and helps you to find inner peace. Some styles are also based on longevity and improving health. There are many different ways to practice the techniques of Taoist meditation and these can be categorized in "Insight," "Visualization," and "Concentrative."

Breathing (Zhuangzi) – With this technique, the main aim is to focus on breathing. Focus on it until it gets extremely soft. You can do this by observing the breath quietly. It is also strikingly similar to Buddhism's mindfulness meditation. It is performed by following the patterns of inhalation and exhalation, so you can be aware of the dynamism of Earth and Heaven.

Emptiness – Here, you will be required to sit calmly and free your mind from all the feelings, thoughts, and images and to forget almost everything in order to experience the inner quiet and emptiness. The "spirit" or the vital force is collected and replenished. It sounds very much similar to "heart-mind fasting".

Beiguan – In this technique, one will need to visualize what is inside your mind and body. This can include the bodily functions inside such as organs and their movements, and even up to the thought processes. This will help you acquaint yourself with the wisdom of your natural body. When doing all the above practices, it helps to perform these while sitting cross-legged with the spine straight. Keep your eyes fixed on the point of the nose and keep them half-closed.

If you are into martial arts like Tai Chi, or if you find yourself to be more connected with nature and the body, then it might do you good to study the philosophy of Taoist meditation.

Chi Kung (Qigong)

Another type of Chinese meditation technique, Qigong refers to "life energy cultivation." In a nutshell, it is a mind/body exercise for meditation, health, and martial arts training. It covers the slow movement of the body, along with it, the regulated use of breathing techniques and its shift towards the attention on inner focus. It was traditionally taught and practiced secretly in the Taoist, Confucianist, and Chinese Buddhist traditions. Later on, it was popularized and incorporated in the 20th century. It also encompasses concentrative exercises and circulation of energy in inner-alchemical mode.

There are about a thousand different ways to perform Qigong exercises, with about 80 types of breathing practices. Some of these are solely dedicated to the martial arts in order to strengthen and energize the body, while others serve to nourish the functions of the body and cure various ailments and diseases. Still, there are others that are for spiritual cultivation and meditation. It can also be practiced in either a standing or seated position or performed through many different movements.

To perform Qigong, one typically assumes a balanced and centered position which is comfortable for you. Next, you must relax all of your nerves, muscles and internal organs. Then try to control your breathing and take long, deep, soft breaths. This will help calm down your mind in the process.

Focus your attention on your body's center of gravity. Just 2 inches below your stomach, also called the lower dantian. This will help you root and accumulate vital energy. Feel the Qi energy as it moves through the body freely. Some of the popular Qigong meditations include Embryonic breathing, Microcosmic circulation, Muscle Tendon changing, and Eight Pieces of Brocade. If you are the active type and you prefer to have more energy for doing physical work, Qigong meditation may be perfect. If you don't like seated meditation and want something more active, there are some dynamic forms you can also try your hand with.

Christian Meditation

Some of the more popular forms of meditation are Hinduism, Jainism, Buddhism, and Taoism. These are widely practiced in the Eastern cultures as a means to attain enlightenment and to help transcend the mind. On the other hand, Christian meditation is founded upon the deeper learning of the Holy Bible and moral purification, establishing the end goal of a deeper connection with Christ. Some of the Christian type of meditations include:

Contemplation – Known as "contemplative reading," as it covers deeps thinking about the events and teachings in the Bible.

Contemplative Prayer – Basically, it covers the silent chanting of sacred sentences and words, with utmost devotion and focus.

Sitting with God – This form of silent meditation is performed in the presence of God while focusing the heart, mind, and soul on contemplation.

Guided Meditations

Towards a greater aspect, the technique of guided meditation is a modern phenomenon. One can easily get started with it by searching for guided meditations influenced by various traditions. It also demands some sort of willpower and determination. Back then, people who were more committed to meditation practiced this type of mediating, because they had very strong sources of motivation. Life had less distractions and people often led more simple lives compared to the busy world of today.

These days, distractions are more, but willpower is less. In this sense, meditation is very important in order to improve performance, have better health, and improve your overall wellbeing. Guided meditation can be a great way to start meditation practice in general, and it can also take your practice to another level once you get started with it. It is something like trying a new recipe and cooking according to a recipe book, that once you know the principles you can then easily cook the dish on your own.

Guided meditation is usually accompanied by a CD, file, or podcast. You can choose any of the following categories of guided meditation below:

Traditional meditation – With the help of an audio, you will be guided by the voice of a teacher in order to focus your attention to be in the meditative state. It has no background music – just a calm, soothing voice to create peace.

Guided Imagery – Here, you will be using your visualization and imagination powers of your brain as it guides you to imagining or visualizing an entity, object, or scenery.

Body scans – Body scans are a great way to achieve deep and intense relaxation in your body. It usually includes soothing nature sounds and instrumental music. It is also often called Yoga Nidra, which is based on calmness and relaxation.

Affirmations – Affirmations are guided imageries with relaxation, and this can help you to imprint a message in your mind.

Binaural Beats – Discovered in the year 1839 by Heinrich Wilhelm Dove, a physicist, this practice believes that the brain identifies the phase exchanges between frequencies when signals of two unique frequencies come individually and it reconciles the change. It also generates alpha waves that are associated with brain waves and it is helpful in the initial level of meditation.

Guided meditations are a great start for those who seem confused where or how to start meditating. It can help with improved self-confidence, coping with a trauma, or if you want to just free your mind of all your stress. There are many techniques in guided imagery that will help you with this.

THE MEDITATION GUIDEBOOK FOR BEGINNERS

Chapter 4: Meditation Posture

Full Lotus

Half Lotus

Burmese

On a stool

Seiza

On a Chair

Perhaps you know a few meditation techniques, but you haven't really begun to practice them because you can't sit still for more than a few minutes, let alone 5, 10, or even 15.

Maybe your back or your knees start hurting, and you worry you may be doing yourself irreparable harm. Or your body starts itching in the oddest places, and you can't resist the urge to scratch. Or every sound reaches your ears magnified a thousandfold — in Dolby stereo, no less — and you start imagining burglars or leaky faucets behind every door.

There Are 6 Traditional Styles Of Sitting:

Full Lotus - Half Lotus - Burmese– are all on the front edge of cushion using the 45% angle of cushion to create natural arch in lower back and keep the chest open. Sitting in a Chair – try not to use the back support- just sit on the front edge of the chair. Kneeling on a cushion on its side – Kneeling on a Stool. Experiment to find what suits you best.

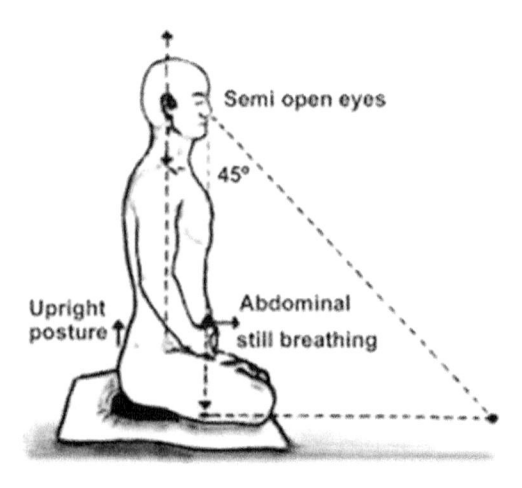

Optimum Meditation Position

A beginner should start with their eyes closed and, as attentional stability increases, you can try meditating with their eyes open, staring at the ground a meter in front of you or even gazing into the space directly in front.

Breathing should be done through the nostrils.

Full lotus

Considered the Everest of sitting positions. With your buttocks on a cushion, cross your left foot over your right thigh and your right foot over your left thigh. As with its more asymmetrical sibling, half lotus, it's best to alternate legs in order to distribute the pressure evenly.

Full lotus has been practiced throughout the world for many thousands of years. The most stable of all the poses, don't attempt it unless you happen to be particularly flexible and even then I suggest preparing by doing some of the stretches described later in this chapter, in the section "Preparing Your Body for Sitting."

Half lotus

The half lotus is easier to execute than the famous full lotus, and nearly as stable. With your buttocks on a cushion, place one foot on the opposite thigh and the other foot on the floor beneath the opposite thigh. Be sure both knees touch the floor and your spine doesn't tilt to one side. To distribute the pressure on your back and legs, remember to alternate legs from sitting to sitting, if you can — in other words, left leg on the thigh and right on the floor, then left on the floor and right on the thigh.

Burmese position

Used throughout Southeast Asia, the Burmese position involves placing both calves and feet on the floor one in front of the other.

Though less stable than the lotus series, it's much easier to negotiate, especially for beginners.

With all the cross-legged poses, first bend your leg at the knee, in line with your thigh, before rotating your thigh to the side. Otherwise, you risk injuring your knee, which is built to flex in only one direction, unlike the ball-and-socket joint of the hip, which can rotate through a full range of motion.

Sitting in a chair

Notice that I say sitting, not slouching. The trick to meditating in a chair is positioning your buttocks somewhat higher than your knees, which tilts your pelvis forward and helps keep your back straight. Old-fashioned wooden kitchen chairs work better than the upholstered kind; experiment with a small cushion or foam wedge under your buttocks.

The seiza pose

Some meditators prefer kneeling instead of sitting. This posture, the seiza pose, originated with Buddhist practitioners in Japan. You place a towel, cushion or soft material between your thighs and calves. Next, assume a kneeling position. Check in with your physical posture and make sure your back is straight and your muscles are relaxed as you begin meditating.

You can kneel on a mat or cushion to support your legs, and many people like to kneel with a meditation bench or cushion under the buttocks to help support and align the back. Comfort is key, so make sure you're comfortable before settling into a meditation posture.

On a stool

A meditation bench is a small, single-person bench that is designed to take the pressure off your legs and ankles when kneeling, and to help keep your back and spine in proper alignment. The bench typically has two short "legs" which may be anywhere from 6-8 inches in height.

These support an angled "seat," where your bottom will sit when you meditate.

To use a meditation bench, you will simply place the bench behind you and get into a kneeling position. Then, you will slide the bench towards your behind. You will keep your ankles flat behind you and move the bench until it's directly above your ankles. Then, sit down and rest your bottom on the seat. If this does not feel comfortable, you can feel free to adjust the angle and position of the bench and your bottom until it feels right.

Tips for a Great Meditation Posture

Let your spine be like a stack of coins.

In classic Buddhist texts the explanation to keep a great posture is to imagine your spine is a stack of coins. Now these instructions may have been before x-rays and chiropractors informing us of the natural curvature of the spine, but the tip still has great value. It gives a nice sense of balance and stability to imagine the stack of coins and if you lean too far forward or back or too far left or right you can easily imagine the coins tumbling over.

Become a puppet on a string.

Imagine you were held up by a string coming from the centre of your crown. Gain a sense of the string lifting you upward. This helps to elongate the spine drawing the energy upward, making you feel lighter and straight. To make this a great posture use your in breath to draw upward being pulled up by the string and use your out breath to relax the shoulders, neck, arms and importantly relax the facial muscles. Use this in and out breath to gain beautiful alignment and relaxation – the benchmarks of a great posture.

Sit like a mountain.

An important element of a good posture is stillness and stability. A great Meditation Masters advice is to sit like a mountain, unmovable, stable and also majestic. Once you have developed alignment and relaxation in your posture imagine you are like a mountain and draw upon that visualisation to help keep you straight and unmovable. Also your posture should be deeply rooted into the earth, grounded and stable. The key here is to remain unmoved and extremely still with the magnificence of huge a mountain.

Find your centre.

A great meditation posture is balanced perfectly in your centre of gravity, it should not be too far forward or back not too far left or right. To get a feel for this centre of balance, after taking your seat, rock your upper body gently around from side to side and front to back and around until you find that place exactly in the middle. This is a great way to relax and let go of tension too and when you get used to doing this you get a feel for you centre and after gently rocking your body naturally comes to rest in the centre.

Let your body reflect your state of mind you are achieving in meditation.

To begin meditation practice you are developing a perfectly balance mind, balanced between not being too tense but also not being too slack. A great meditation posture reflects a state of mind of being alert and relaxed at the same time. The too biggest obstacles to a balanced and calm mind is over excitement – thinking too much and drowsiness or sluggishness. A great posture helps to combat these two obstacles by reflecting the perfect balance of being upright and alert and being relaxed and comfortable.

Perfect symmetry.

A great meditation posture is symmetrical. Your right side of your body should be a mirror image of the left. This is especially relevant for knees and shoulders. Adjust your posture so your knees are at the same height and shoulders are perfectly even as well. Keep your hands in your lap or on your knees but make sure they are a mirror image of each other. Let someone take a picture of you while you are in your meditation posture so you can see clearly where the further adjustments can be made.

Qualities of a Good Meditation Position

A meditation posture should include three main qualities:

Alignment

Alignment of the back, neck and head in a comfortable upright natural way, do not hunch, do not lean neck forward, simply sit up straight' with the chin slightly lowered. To help with alignment imagine a string attached from the centre of the crown and you are being drawn upward. Also try and raise the chest slightly to prevent slumping.

Relaxation

Relaxation of muscles, particularly the neck, shoulders and face. The posture should be comfortable. The arms should hang effortlessly, with the hands resting in the lap or lightly on the knees. The legs should be comfortable and relaxed and if your knees do not touch the ground you can support them with extra cushions to ease any pain in the hips.

Stillness

Stillness of body means stability, not easily moved, with a sense of balance. To find your centre of balance you can gently rock side to side and forward and backward until you find a sense of the middle of your posture. For the duration of the meditation it is important to sit very still.

Eyes can be closed, slightly open or completely open, but should always remain fixed and not moving around, even when closed. You can experiment with both open and closed eyes. When open gaze at the floor 1-2 meters in front of you on the floor.

Experimentation is encouraged and always remember the point of a meditation posture is not to torture yourself with pain; if persistent pain occurs, try sitting in a chair, using a meditation stool or even lying flat on the floor.

Remember the posture should be straight but also relaxed, which represents and reflects the meditative state of mind of being alert yet calm.

"A good meditation posture is very still, balanced and comfortable."

Chapter 5: Meditation for the Body Chakra

According to yogic theory, the body contains seven primary energy centers called chakras. These centers of energy roughly correspond to the spine and nervous system centers in anatomy. They are beyond definition, though they are psycho-spiritual centers through which life-force energy travels. The Saturn chakra is located at the base of your spine, and in it lies a powerful but often dormant energy source.

Yoga philosophy calls this source of energy kundalini energy, and compares it to a snake lying coiled and sleeping inside every person. Awakening this energy causes it to rise up through the chakras. When it reaches the top chakra, located at the crown of the skull, you may be able to realize and grasp your full potential and become enlightened about the unity of all things.

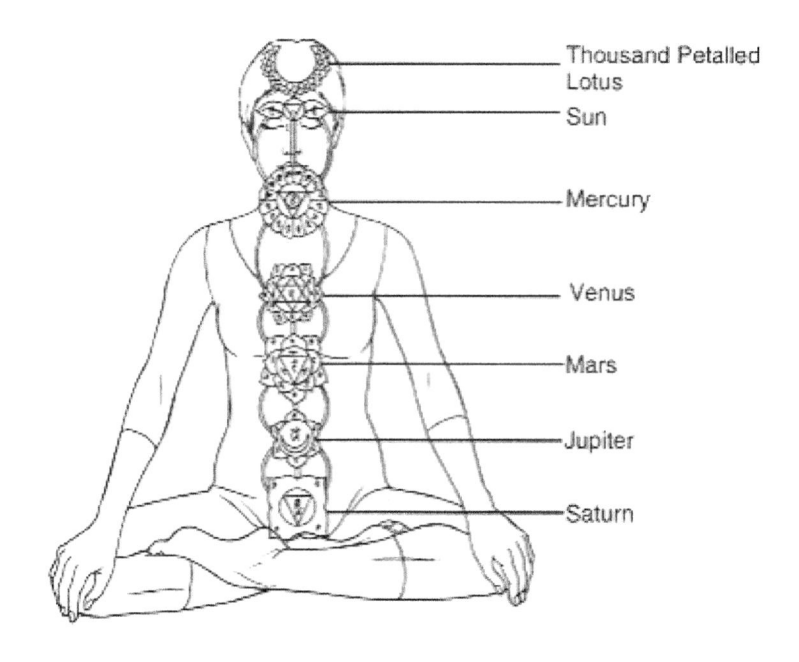

Meditation on the Chakras

Chakras are psycho-spiritual energy centers in the body. The seven major chakras are:

- ✓ The Saturn, or Muladhara, chakra at the base of the spine (source of dormant energy)
- ✓ The Jupiter, or Swadhishthana, chakra behind the lower abdomen (source of creative energy and passion)
- ✓ The Mars, or Manipura, chakra behind the navel (source of action energy and of the digestive fire)
- ✓ The Venus, or Anahata, chakra behind the heart (source of compassionate energy and emotion)
- ✓ The Mercury, or Vishuddha, chakra in the throat (source of communication energy)

- ✓ The Sun, or Ajna, chakra on the forehead at the site of the urna, or third eye (source of intuitive energy, unclouded perception, and intuition)

The Thousand Petalled Lotus, or Sahasrara chakra, at the crown of the head (source of enlightenment energy and self-realization)

Each (and every) chakra can become blocked, and certain exercises, such as yoga postures, can help to open them.

Meditation, too, can help to open them. If you're feeling blocked (or even if you would just like to enhance your energy in a certain area), try one or two or all of our chakra meditations.

Saturn Chakra: Coiled Energy

The Saturn chakra lies at the base of your spine, where kundalini energy waits to be awakened. While sitting comfortably, close your eyes and focus your attention on the base of your spine. Sense the Earth beneath you. Feel the connection between your Saturn chakra and the ground below. Feel the Earth's energy powering your Saturn chakra and merging with your kundalini energy. Imagine this energy flowing slowly up your spine and out each of your limbs.

Imagine it flowing upward out of the crown of your head. Imagine the energy pulsing and flashing, flushing and suffusing you with crackling, spectacular power. Now, allow the energy to dissipate slowly, falling back, leaving you energized but calm. Bring the energy back down into your Saturn chakra, ready to be activated when you need it. Feel again your connection with the Earth's energy. Breathe.

The Saturn chakra connects you with the Earth beneath you.

Jupiter Chakra: Creation Energy

The Jupiter chakra is associated with creative energy and passion.

Your Jupiter chakra is located in your lower abdomen. It is the seat of your creative energy. Sitting comfortably, close your eyes and focus your attention on your Jupiter chakra. Imagine your life-force energy concentrating in your lower abdomen. Imagine it intensifying, looking for an outlet. The energy builds, then transforms into pure creativity.

Imagine this creativity mobilizing and flowing through your body, into your brain. Imagine it filling and activating your brain, preparing you to use it for whatever purpose you require. You become pure creativity. You can do anything. Breathe and imagine that creative energy stilling, holding, waiting for instructions. Open your eyes. Now go create something!

Mars Chakra: Action Energy

Your Mars chakra is located behind your navel. It is the seat of action energy. Sitting comfortably, close your eyes and focus your attention on your Mars chakra. Breathe deeply, and with each breath, imagine that energy is flowing from the air around you and from the Earth below you into your Mars chakra, where the energy accumulates.

Imagine it stirring and swirling and sparking. Consciously release this energy into the rest of your body. Feel it flowing down your legs and into your feet. Feel it flooding your chest and streaming down your arms. Feel your hands and fingers tingling. Imagine it flowing into your head and awakening your brain.

Imagine your hair standing on end, energy streaming out of your scalp. Feel the energy straightening your spine, activating your muscles, and awakening your mind. Now, open your eyes slowly and feel how energized you are. The rest of your day should be a breeze!

THE MEDITATION GUIDEBOOK FOR BEGINNERS

The Mars chakra is the seat of action energy.

Venus Chakra: Heart Energy

The Venus chakra is associated with compassionate energy.

Your Venus chakra is located behind your heart. It is the seat of compassionate energy. Sitting comfortably, close your eyes and focus your attention on your Venus chakra.

Breathe, and with each breath, imagine pure love streaming from your heart into the world. With your first 10 breaths, send compassion and love into the room where you are meditating. With the next 10 breaths, imagine the compassionate energy flooding out the doors to fill your entire house or apartment. With the next 10 breaths, imagine the love energy overflowing your house or apartment, spilling out the windows and doors and encompassing your neighborhood.

The next 10 breaths flood your town or city with compassionate energy. The next 10 breaths fill your state. With the next 10 breaths, compassionate energy flows over the entire country. Then, the continent. With the last 10 breaths, embrace the entire planet in love. You can even extend out beyond the Earth to the other planets, galaxies, and realms of existence. Feel how strong and far-reaching your energy can be.

Before you know it, compassionate energy will start bouncing back to you.

Mercury Chakra: Communication Energy

The Mercury chakra is associated with communication.

Your Mercury chakra is located in your throat. It is the seat of communication. Sitting comfortably, close your eyes and focus your attention on your Mercury chakra. Breathe and imagine your throat opening. Consider how you tend to communicate, then imagine that when your Mercury chakra is open, you can communicate effortlessly, speaking to others in a way that perfectly expresses your thoughts.

Imagine the power of communication flowing from the universe, God, or whatever source makes sense to you, into your Mercury chakra, and then back out of you. Contemplate the way Ghandi, the Buddha, Moses, Mohammed, and other gifted spiritual leaders were able to communicate with divine and inspirational simplicity. You, too, have the ability to communicate at much deeper levels.

Sun Chakra: The Third Eye

The Sun chakra, or third eye, is the seat of perceptive energy and unclouded thinking.

Your Sun chakra, or third eye, is located on your forehead, between and just above your eyes. It is the seat of perceptive energy and unclouded thinking. Try this one outside on a sunny day, if possible. Sitting comfortably (try a blanket, quilt, or mat on the grass), close your eyes and tilt your face toward the sun. Focus your attention on your Sun chakra and imagine yourself communicating with the sun.
Feel its rays flowing directly into your Sun chakra. Imagine your Sun chakra opening and instead of being blinded by the sun, imagine you can suddenly see everything with a clarity you've never experienced

before. With your eyes still closed, imagine looking around you and seeing your house, your yard, or whatever your surroundings are, in an entirely new light - the light of the enlightened sun and the light of unclouded perception.

How do things look? Sharper, more beautiful, radiating energy? How would you see the people in your life when looking at them through your Sun chakra? Now, open your eyes slowly. Do things look different than before? You may actually be seeing more clearly.

Thousand Petalled Lotus: Enlightenment.

The Thousand Petalled Lotus is the chakra located at the crown of your head. It is the seat of enlightenment energy. Sitting comfortably, close your eyes and focus your attention on your Thousand Petalled Lotus. Imagine it opening slowly, like the petals of a flower just beginning to bloom. Quietly repeat to yourself the words All is one. Say them slowly, hearing the way they sound, contemplating what they mean. Say it again and again until you feel as if your Thousand Petalled Lotus is opening in full and magnificent bloom. Ommmm.

The Thousand Petalled Lotus is the chakra of bliss, the enlightenment energy.

Your Aura Is Showing!

With all this energy flowing around and through you, wouldn't you think you might be able to see it? Actually, according to some, you can. Anyone can. All you have to do is develop your auric sight.

Although their existence is controversial, many believe that auras are the visual result of the vibrations that surround every material object. People have them, objects have them, plants, animals, trees, even articles of clothing, kitchen utensils, and bodies of water. Scientists will tell you that everything is made up of atoms, molecules, electrons, etc., and that these subcomponents of existence are by no means solid or still. They are filled with space and they move. So it makes sense that we are vibrating creatures, down to the atomic level.

We also emit electromagnetic energy. We emit heat. And some of that energy is emitted as ultraviolet light.

According to auric theory, the part of our energy emitted as ultraviolet light is the part related to our consciousness, emotions, intentions, and spirituality. Auras, especially around the head, can reveal someone's basic character, mood at the moment, level of spiritual attainment, and even whether or not they are telling the truth.

The color of an aura is indicative of a person's basic mental, emotional, and spiritual state. Bright, clear colors mean a person is well intentioned, has a good nature, and is spiritually advanced. Dark, muddy, or cloudy colors denote bad intentions, materialistic natures, dark or depressed thoughts, pain, or anger. Auras can also contain little shoots and bursts of color within them. For example, bursts of purple are indicative of spiritual thoughts.

Chakras Have Colors, Too

Every chakra is associated with a color, and many claim that with practice, you can actually see a person's chakra glowing with that color. For example, the Sun chakra (or third eye) in the middle of the forehead appears a deep indigo. The more colorful and glowing the color, the more spiritual the person.

Each chakra is associated with the following color (although be aware that different people may associate the chakras with different colors than we do, and different colors mean different things to different people). Feel free to add these colors to your chakra meditations.

✓ Thousand Petalled Lotus	Violet
✓ Sun chakra	Indigo
✓ Mercury chakra	Blue
✓ Venus chakra	Green
✓ Mars chakra	Yellow
✓ Jupiter chakra	Orange
✓ Saturn chakra	Red

A Special Way of Seeing

Learning to see an aura isn't difficult, but it becomes even easier with practice. Experienced auric-seers barely have to concentrate to see someone's aura, and the colors and subcolors are obvious and clear. Like to give it a try?

We'll teach you how to see your own aura. Then, you can also apply the same technique to look at someone else's aura.

Here's how it works:

Stand about four or five feet from a large mirror. The wall or surface behind you should be white or off-white (any solid, unmarked light color will do, but white is easiest). Lighting should be adequate but not too bright, and the surface behind you should be evenly lit without bright spots or shadows.

Fix your eyes on the reflection of your Sun chakra, that point between and about one or two inches up from your eyes (the third eye).

Gaze at that point for one full minute without moving your eyes away. You can blink, but don't look anywhere else. Then, still without moving your eyes away from that point, survey the area around your head via your peripheral vision. It might be hard to see at first, and you might be tempted to look directly at it, but don't. It works best if you keep your eyes fixed to your third eye. Eventually, you should see a sort of halo or illuminated area around your head. That is your aura. Notice the color or colors you see.

The first time you try this exercise, you may only be able to keep it up for a couple of minutes, but if you gradually increase your time to 10 or 15 minutes per day, you'll get better and better. You'll be able to see auras everywhere.

But what do the aura colors mean? Maybe your aura was a beautiful sky blue, a pale turquoise, or a sunny yellow.

Different sources interpret colors in different ways, and so to some extent, only you can interpret the color of your aura and what it means (even though many people out there will be happy to interpret your aura for you, for a fee, of course). There are a few basic characteristics that many people agree belong to different colors, however. I'll give you some generalizations, but your instinct about why your particular aura is blue, orange, or yellow at the particular moment is probably the most accurate.

Aura Color Qualities

- ✓ Blue — Calm, relaxed, tranquil, maternal, attentive, and caring
- ✓ Brown — Unspiritual, unsettled, anxious, nervous, distracted
- ✓ Gray — Depressed, pessimistic, negative, repressed anger
- ✓ Green — Intelligent, straightforward, natural healer, quick thinker, close to nature, a doer
- ✓ Orange — Creative, inspiring, compassionate, powerful, able to inspire and/or manipulate people

- ✓ Pink — Protected, dominated by pure and radiant love
- ✓ Purple/violet — Spiritual, intuitive, psychic abilities, dedicated to leading humanity toward the next step in higher consciousness
- ✓ Red — Physical, materialistic, passionate, easily excited, emphasis on the body, intense emotion
- ✓ Sulfur-colored — Discomfort, pain, irritation, festering anger
- ✓ Turquoise — Full of energy, natural leader, organized
- ✓ White — Innocence, purity, spirituality, or serious illness, altered state due to artificial substances
- ✓ Yellow — Joyful, playful, blissful; when gold, rare spiritual development, highly evolved

Some aura theorists believe that all young children and infants can clearly see auras, but they lose this natural ability as they age. Another theory is that in past ages, more people could see auras and that in paintings, halos around saints and religious figures, such as Jesus and the Buddha, were actually auras perceived by the artists.

Aura theorists often advise that anyone claiming to be a spiritual leader should have a bright golden-yellow aura. If they don't, they shouldn't be trusted as spiritual guides. Legend has it both Jesus and the Buddha had large golden auras around their heads, and expansive pink auras around their entire bodies, suggesting spiritual perfection.

During the 1940s, a Russian photographer developed a photographic technique through which energy fields could actually be documented. Kurlian's images of both objects and people were stunning, and proof to many that auras do exist and that energy-based healing therapies are actually based on something real and measurable. One image of a leaf cut in half revealed an energy field that still surrounded the entire leaf.

People who have experienced amputation often experience pain in the amputated area, and stories abound of bodyworkers who manipulated the energy over where the missing limb would have been and are able to elicit positive results in their patients.

Chapter 6: The Art of Aura Meditation – An Exercise

Although auras tend to have a primary color reflecting someone's basic nature, they also change according to mood, health, and other factors. Some people believe you can actually alter the color of your aura through concentration. Aura meditation is a great way to adjust your aura to a healthful and productive state. It also offers a great point of focus for your concentration.

Try the following aura meditation exercise after you've spent a few weeks practicing how to find your own aura and feel comfortable doing so. It should take 20 to 30 minutes:

Sit down comfortably about four or five feet in front of a mirror so that you are backed by a light-colored background. You can use a chair or you can sit on the floor.

Find your third eye (as instructed above) and fix your gaze upon it. Breathe normally but listen to your breath.

Concentrate all your energy on that one spot on your forehead for one full minute. After a minute is up (don't look at a watchdon't move those eyesbut you can count off 60 seconds to yourself as you concentrate), find your aura by using your peripheral vision. Notice its color.

Now think about blue. Blue is the color of relaxation and balance. Imagine your entire body relaxing. Imagine a brilliant blue color washing over your entire being, dissolving muscle tension and all your worries, washing them away in sapphire waves of blue. Keep your eyes fixed on your third eye, but think blue, blue, blue. Try to adjust your aura to become bluer, brighter, and clearer. Stay with blue for at least five minutes.

Now, think about green. Imagine that your body is now so relaxed that it is ready and able to heal itself. Imagine that all things amiss in your system, from a stuffy nose to a scrape on your knee, allergies, high blood pressure, arthritis, or whatever, are open and ready for healing. Green is the color of natural healing abilities.

Visualize a beautiful, grassy green color flowing over your body. Breathe it in and out. Notice how green feels as it moves through you, knitting, repairing, unblocking, flushing, and calming your system into a more healthful state. Try to adjust your aura to become greener, brighter, and clearer. Stay with green for at least five minutes.

Now, think about yellow. Yellow is the color of pure joy. Imagine your body immersed in a brilliant column of sunny yellow light. This light dissolves all your sorrows, all your attachments, everything that causes you to feel sadness or suffering. Imagine yellow flowing through you, filling you with joy, bliss, and a playful spirit.

Now imagine the yellow column of light is shot through with showers of sparkling, gleaming gold. Imagine your higher self emerging, merging with the universe in a transcendent yet warmly familiar unity. Feel as if you are finally at home. Let the smile show on your face. Feel the bliss. Is your aura shimmering?

Bask in gold for a while, then briefly recall the feel of yellow, green, and blue. Breathe deeply for another minute or two, then close your eyes. You'll see the imprint of your aura for a couple of seconds. Bid it farewell, open your eyes, and move on with your day, at peace.

Natural Medicine Goes with the Flow

It's great to learn how to direct your own energy, but maybe you have a true gift for healing and could help heal the energy of others. Many are doing just that, practicing different forms of healing and bodywork to help re-align and replenish life-force energy in others, as well as teaching others to replenish and manage their own energy. Techniques abound, but here are a few of the most popular.

Reiki

Pronounced ray-kee, Reiki is a type of bodywork that emphasizes the manipulation of life-force energy through the chakras. The Reiki practitioner places his or her hands on the receiver over the chakras, working along the front and the back of the body. Each touch is held for several minutes, allowing universal life-force energy to flow through the practitioner into the receiver (the energy comes from the universe, not from the Reiki practitioner, who serves as a channel, not as an energy source).

The theory is that chakras are special places on the body where energy can enter, and placing hands over them allows them to open and receive energy. The more energy in the body, the better it can heal, align, and balance itself.

There are several levels of Reiki accomplishment, culminating in the title of Reiki Master. Training involves a process that unblocks the practitioner's own chakras so they can serve as ideal energy channelers.

Although you can't learn Reiki from a book alone, try the following Reiki meditation. The area you are holding is your point of concentration. Remember those chakras? Work through each one, holding your hands over the area for about three minutes each. As you hold your hands over your chakras, imagine tapping life-force energy from the universe and feel it flowing into your chakras, suffusing your body and soul with vitality:

Reiki I
Self Healing hand positions

Pos 1. Pos 2. Pos 3. Pos 4. Pos 5.
Pos 6. Pos 7. Pos 8. Pos 9. Pos 10.
(Pos Optional) Pos 11. Pos 12 a. Pos 12 b. (Pos 12 Alternative)
Pos 13. Pos 14. Pos 15 (Pos Optional)
Pos 16. Pos 17. Pos 16 b. Pos 17 b.

- ✓ Sit or stand comfortably with your back straight. Place the fingers of both hands along your eyebrows with your little fingers resting on the bridge of your nose. Your palms should be cupping your cheeks. Press very gently with your fingers around the eyes. Hold.

- ✓ Place your palms on either side of your head so your fingers barely touch across the crown of your head. Hold.
- ✓ Reach around to the back of your head and, fingers barely touching, cradle the back of your skull. Hold.
- ✓ Next, place your right hand gently on your throat and your left hand across the top of your sternum so that the fingers of your left hand rest beneath the wrist of your right hand. Hold.
- ✓ Now place your palms on your lower chest near the bottom ribs. Hold.
- ✓ Place your palms over your stomach so your fingers touch over your navel. Hold.
- ✓ Place your palms over your lower abdomen with your fingers pointing diagonally downward and touching just over your pubic bone. Hold.
- ✓ Place your hands over your shoulders behind you and press your palms against your upper back, fingers pointed down. Hold.
- ✓ Bend your left arm behind you and rest your hand over your right shoulder blade. Hold. Repeat on the other side. Hold.
- ✓ Place both hands around your lower ribcage on your back, just above your waist. Hold.
- ✓ Place both hands over the tops of your hip bones on your back, just above your buttocks. Hold.
- ✓ Now, bring your hands back to the front and cup your right hand in your left hand. Breathe in and out naturally for another three minutes, feeling the life-force energy moving through your body, flushing away negativity and replacing it with healing and joy.

Acupuncture

Acupuncture is a centuries-old technique that originated in China. Hair-thin needles are inserted into pressure points for pain relief and healing. The theory goes that by stimulating pressure points, acupuncture releases blocked areas and equalizes life-force energy, allowing the body to solve its own pain and heal itself. Some people meditate during their acupuncture treatments to facilitate the process.

Many insurance companies in the United States now cover acupuncture treatments, and although many mainstream physicians admit they don't know why it works, they also admit that it does work. Before receiving treatment, make sure you find an acupuncturist who is properly trained and licensed.

Therapeutic Touch

Therapeutic Touch (TT) is a controversial technique in which patients are treated by practitioners who never touch them. The theory behind TT is similar to the theory behind Reiki: life-force energy can become imbalanced, and the TT therapist acts as a channel for life-force energy to flow into the receiver. However, in TT, the practitioner's hands usually stay about four to six inches above the skin of the receiver, touching only the body's energy field.

Some practitioners even incorporate guided visualizations, transforming the session into a sort of mind-body meditation.

Chapter 7: Where to Meditate

So you're under stress. What a shocker! What else is new in the modern world? Right now, you're probably good and ready to start doing something about it, so let's get down to some practical details that'll help you establish a regular, structured meditation practice.

In this chapter we'll help you find the perfect place to meditate. Technically, you can meditate anywhere, but there's no question that some places are more conducive to meditation than others. We'd like to help you survey the space you have and guide you in the creation of a perfect meditation space that is all your own.

Creating a Meditation Space in Your Home

Ideally, you could devote an entire room in your home to meditation, making it into a spiritual sanctuary.

Unfortunately, not many people have an extra room to spare for this purpose. (If you happen to be in the process of designing a house to build, however, why not consider adding a small meditation room?) If you live in a limited space, however (like most of us), that doesn't mean you can't carve out the perfect spot for your daily meditation.

First, let's look at what's available in your home. Take the following list and walk through every room in your house. Check any spaces that might make possible meditation spaces:

Living Room/Den:

- ✓ Is your living room or den L-shaped? Could one end of the L be set apart with a curtain or stand-up screen for meditation?
- ✓ Do you have a spacious coat closet? Do you really use it, or could coats be relocated to an attractive coat rack or set of hooks by the door?
- ✓ Do you have any small areas like nooks, window seats, or closets?
- ✓ Do you have a home office or separate den that isn't completely full or only used occasionally?

Kitchen/Dining Room:

- ✓ Do you have an enclosed pantry? Could you clean it out, throw out all the junk, and relocate food to the kitchen cabinets?
- ✓ Do you have a breakfast nook set off from the main kitchen?
- ✓ Do you have an enclosed formal dining room that rarely gets used?

Bedrooms/Bathrooms:

- ✓ Do you have a walk-in closet? Could clothes and shoes be relocated to a shallower closet or a stand-alone wardrobe?
- ✓ Any window seats, nooks, or extra floor space you could surround with a drape or stand-up screens?

- ✓ Is your bathroom extra-large and comfortable (one of those bathrooms that is more room than bath)? Could you devote a corner to meditation?
- ✓ Do you have a guestroom that isn't regularly occupied?

- ✓ Indoor/Outdoor:

- ✓ Do you have a large screened-in porch or small porch that isn't used much?
- ✓ Do you have a garage or garden shed that isn't overwhelmed with junk or that could be cleaned out and made comfortable?
- ✓ Any balconies, decks, or roof areas made to walk on?
- ✓ Do you have a beautiful garden, tree or group of trees, corner of a hedge, or water source that would make an aesthetically appealing spot for meditation?
- ✓ Are there any unattached structures, such as gazebos, arches, arbors, trellises, or even a fenced-in corner or niche?

Now look at your list and the items you checked. Which seem the most practical, and also, the most private? Think about which area you'd like to use, talk to other family members about it if necessary, and get to work making the space your own.

Meditation Doesn't Mean Deprivation!

Once you've chosen a meditation space, the next step is personalization. Maybe you thought meditation was the stuff of ascetics and your meditation space must be spartan. Far from it! In fact, for the beginning meditator, comfort is extremely important. Otherwise, you may be setting yourself up to give up before you even get started.

How do you make your meditation space comfortable? First, it would help if you could regulate the temperature. If you can't or if you like to meditate outside, keep a soft blanket or quilt nearby to wrap yourself in. Hypothermia during meditation may help keep you awake, but it sure isn't conducive to sitting in one place for 20 minutes or more!

Likewise, if your meditation space is too hot, the heat will probably become distracting. Make sure the area has sufficient ventilation. Although natural cooling is preferable (open windows and fans, for example) during mid-summer, especially in warmer climates, we'll admit the A/C can feel really good. If blasting the air conditioner is the only way you can stand to sit there, then by all means, blast away.

Setting Up

Next, consider aesthetics. Maybe the only space you can find to be alone is the attic, the basement, or the garage.

That's great—unless just looking at these places depresses you. If your meditation space is cluttered with junk, you'll have a hard time clearing your mind. Our surroundings are often reflective of our internal housekeeping and changing our surroundings can alter our internal sense of ourselves. So before you meditate in your meditation space, make sure the space is ready.

First, you'll want to clean your space really well. Clean from top to bottom and everything in between. Get rid of cobwebs, sort through junk and organize, throw away everything that you haven't used for one year and that doesn't have any significant personal meaning for you. Sweep, scrub, scour, polish, and shine.

You also might want to consider cleansing the energies of the room:

First, make sure the space is immaculately clean.

- ✓ Open a window, a door, or both, so negative energy has somewhere to go.
- ✓ Declare your intention by standing or sitting in the middle of the room and concentrating on cleansing the energies of the room for the purpose of making it a spiritual space, a relaxing space, or both. If it helps, speak your intention out loud: It will cleanse the energies of this room to make it a suitable space for meditation.
- ✓ Walk slowly around the room with a burning incense stick or smudge with a sage smudge stick, waving it into all the corners and crannies where energy could get stuck. (You can buy smudge sticks at many organic grocery or health-food stores and other shops and boutiques that carry meditation tools.)
- ✓ Begin in the middle of the room and walk in a spiral as you ring a bell. The sound waves from the bell can purify the energy. Keep walking a tight spiral until you are walking around the edges of the room. Repeat if the sound of the bell still sounds muffled. You can

- even clear the space by walking around the room clapping your hands.
- ✓ You'll also want the place to have the right ambience. Light candles, burn incense, play relaxing music. Decorate with colors that make you feel tranquil (blues and greens are good) or joyful (orange and yellow are good). Hang the walls with tapestries or pictures showing symbols, figures, or scenes that relax and inspire you. You can even construct a personal altar on which you keep items of spiritual significance to you.
- ✓ Personal altars can provide you with a sense that your meditation space is truly yours. They can also provide items to use as points of concentration during meditation and can inspire you to maintain a reverent and spiritual frame of mind. All your altar need be is a small table, shelf, or cabinet. Fill it with items that mean something to you:
- ✓ If you feel close to nature, keep pinecones, seashells, fresh flowers, pine branches, glass bowls of seawater, a miniature fountain, even a small fish tank on your altar.
- ✓ If you're devoted to a specific religion, keep statues, sacred texts, symbols, or other representations of those beliefs on your altar. (For example, statues of Buddha, of Hindu gods like Krishna or Ganesha, a crucifix or picture of Jesus, a Bible, a cross, a picture of the Om symbol, etc.)
- ✓ If you are inspired by music, keep a collection of instruments on your altar: small flutes, chimes, gongs, drums, whistles, rattles, and bells.

- ✓ If you are inspired by art, cover your altar with prints, photos, sculptures, or paintings you find meaningful and inspiring.
- ✓ If you admire and emulate a particular spiritual leader, include a picture of him or her on your altar.

If you feel centered and grounded by considering the four elements, keep a bowl of water, a stick of burning incense or a burning candle (for fire), a bowl of salt or a beautiful crystal (for earth), and a wind chime (for air) on your altar.

Sounds, Sights, and Smells

Ideally, meditation involves withdrawal of the senses. Complete sense withdrawal isn't easy, however, especially for beginners. In fact, your senses can actually work for you, to help you train yourself to concentrate. The trick is not to bombard them, but to focus on them one at a time.

To help with this pursuit, you can fill your meditation space with tools and equipment that can help you with concentration techniques. You can spend thousands of dollars on fancy meditation and relaxation tools, but you needn't spend a penny. Consider some of the following:

- ✓ A cassette or CD player to play relaxing, tranquil music such as classical music or any of the many CDs designed for relaxation or meditation.
- ✓ A wind chime hung near an open window or in the current of a fan.

- ✓ Small mechanical fountains to provide the peaceful sound of flowing water. The sounds of bells, gongs, chimes, rattles, flutes, and drums can all be used as points of focus.
- ✓ Light/sound devices consisting of computerized glasses or masks that provide a light and sound show designed to ease the brain into a relaxed state.
- ✓ Candles, candles, candles, for use as a point of focus and also to give the room a warm glow.
- ✓ Mandala artwork, other spiritually inspired artwork.
- ✓ Incense and incense burner.
- ✓ Essential oil warmers or diffusers.
- ✓ Drape walls with fabric in tranquil colors (but keep any draped fabric away from candles and incense!).

Honoring Your Meditation Space

Once you've created your meditation space to be a true embodiment of you (not of some generic idea you have about meditation), it should feel comfortable, not foreign or strange. Entering it should fill you with tranquility and satisfaction. If your intention is to have a relaxing space, your space should make you feel relaxed just stepping into it. If your intention is to have a spiritual haven, you should feel spiritually inspired by your space.

Meditation room. surrounded by sky and Nature, the room is blue in color to evoke the peacefulness of a natural setting and sparsely furnished. Candles for soft lighting, plants, and moveable pillows create a functional and calming environment. A window allows for fresh air.

Now that you've crafted your space, honor it. Keep it sparkling clean. Periodically replace burned-down candles and wilted flowers. Clean up incense ash, shake out pillows and mats, dust your altar. Also, every so often, especially when you seem to have hit a meditation plateau, cleanse the energy of your space again, as directed above. Remember to open the windows and doors.

Also, when in your meditation space, you can honor it and maintain the atmosphere by behaving with reverence.

Take your shoes off at the door. Speak softly. You might even consider saying a blessing each time you enter or exit the door or entrance to the space. A few to try:

- ✓ I honor this space.
- ✓ Thank you for this haven.
- ✓ May truth be present here.

Feng Shui: Beneficial Energies for Your Home

The ancient art of Feng Shui (pronounced fung shway) originated in China thousands of years ago but has become suddenly in. Feng Shui is the art of arranging interiors, furniture and other items and landscaping to make them more conducive to greater health, prosperity, love, spirituality, or other higher goals.

Donald Trump hires experts to decorate his buildings using Feng Shui techniques. Bookstores are brimming with books on Feng Shui and in most cities you can find a Feng Shui master to help you arrange your living space to best facilitate the flow of energy.

The idea makes sense: Just as bodies contain life-force energy that flows through certain channels, the rest of the world flows with energy, too. Call it prana, chi, or whatever you like. It's everywhere, and it enlivens our cities, our towns, our neighborhoods, our homes, our workplaces, our gardens, and our meditation spaces. Or if those spaces are arranged so that they block and stagnate or drain the energy, it deadens them.

I won't pretend to be Feng Shui masters, but we can tell you a couple of basic principles you can use in your meditation space (and in your home, too). In general, keep in mind that energy is affected by everything around it, including objects and also including the moods, attitudes, emotions, and actions of the people it surrounds. (Another reason to behave with reverence in your meditation space!)

Also keep in mind that although general principles do exist, Feng Shui is to some extent an individual matter.

Arrange things so they feel right to you, even if you don't know why. Trust your instinct.

Try the following Feng Shui techniques in your meditation space:

- ✓ Placing mirrors in corners, nooks, and other spaces where swirling energy could become trapped helps to loosen the energy and keep it moving.
- ✓ Living things (plants, fish, flowers, pine branches, etc.) and clean crystals help draw in energy and keep it moving.
- ✓ Square shapes hold energy while round shapes move energy (so you might consider a square altar in a round room, or a square meditation mat or pillow with pictures of round mandalas on the walls).
- ✓ Keep the area outside the door or entrance to your meditation space clear (also the space outside the door to your home) so energy has an open channel through which to enter the room. Also, if your door

opens to a wall, place a mirror on the wall to push the energy into the room.
- ✓ Your kitchen is indicative of your financial situation. A dirty kitchen (especially a dirty stove) indicates financial problems.
- ✓ Corners, beams, pillars, posts, and large pieces of furniture in the middle of rooms disturb energy flow. Keep the space clear and give energy a river to flow through.
- ✓ The ideal place in your home for a meditation space is the lower-left corner when standing in the entranceway of your house. This is the part of the house related to self-realization, introspection, and meditation. The center of the house is also good. This space represents health and energy.
- ✓ Crystals hanging in the windows focus and intensify energy.

Creating Outdoor Meditation Spaces: Sacred Geometry

If your meditation space is outside, you can still make certain changes to create the perfectly personalized meditation space. Filling your yard with living plants, flowers, and trees will bring it to life, even if you only have space for potted plants. Limit or eliminate the use of chemical pesticides and fertilizers.

Try organic gardening methods instead to have a truly Earth-friendly space. And whenever you get the chance, plant a tree. Trees are like wise old souls and make excellent meditation partners. You'll feel grounded sitting over those deep roots and sheltered by the tree canopy.

Zen Gardening

Zen gardening can be as easy as filling a bowl with sand and rocks, and as comprehensive as specially landscaping your entire property. Zen gardens are meant to serve as meditation spaces. They typically reflect the ideas and spirit of the culture, so your Zen garden should reflect you more than, say, Japan (unless you are from Japan, in which case it could do both!). Zen gardens are typically dry, and use sand and rocks to represent water. Sand represents the ocean, and plants or trees could represent vast forests. Dry streambeds made with stone are a common feature.

Sand may also be raked in geometric patterns. Zen gardens are miniature representations of natural or spiritual phenomena.

Before crafting your own Zen garden, think about what you would want your meditation space to represent. How could you represent your ideas, your self, in a garden?

But sand in a bowl designed with circles and streams of pebbles or raked in patterns can be a Zen garden, too, and a garden this small could fit on your personal altar.

Take a look at Chapter 27, Om Away from Om: Spiritual Travel, where you'll find many sacred places discussed, including Japanese Zen gardens.

Pond and Water Spaces

Water can be inspiring, grounding, uplifting, refreshing, and purifying. The sound of water makes an excellent point of focus for meditation, and the sight of a bubbling fountain, a pond surrounded by flowers and filled with bright orange koi (large Japanese goldfish), or even a beautiful birdbath can be the perfect addition to an outdoor meditation space. Check your local garden center for supplies. Many companies also sell water gardening equipment of fine quality in unique designs.

Chapter 8: When to Meditate

Meditating at random times each day is better than no meditation, but it isn't ideal, either. Many philosophies postulate that a regular schedule is best for a calm mind and good health. For example, Indian Ayurveda prescribes a regular routine for people who suffer from health problems, which they see as imbalances of internal forces.

If you're schedule-resistant, adopting a regular schedule may seem impossible and even undesirable. Maybe you like your free-wheelin' lifestyle! But a regular time for meditation, if for nothing else, will help to keep you grounded and centered. Although you may at first dread anything you have to do every day at a certain time, look at it as a welcome oasis rather than a chore or a burden. Sure, sometimes you won't feel like it. But discipline is the first step to freedom. (Really!)

To find the ideal meditation time for you, check the items in the following list that apply to you:

Energy Factor:

- ✓ My energy peak seems to be in the early morning.
- ✓ My energy peak seems to be in the late morning.
- ✓ My energy peak seems to be in the afternoon.
- ✓ My energy peak seems to be in the early evening.

✓ My energy peak seems to be late at night.

Time Factor:

- ✓ I have to be at work very early in the morning.
- ✓ I get home at least an hour or two before dinner.
- ✓ I have a free space in the middle of the day.
- ✓ I am completely swamped with responsibility until everyone goes to sleep at night.

Believe it or not, it is better to meditate during times of peak energy than in times of low energy. Even though your meditation practice may involve sitting or lying down, you'll need a lot of energy to channel into the effort of mindfulness, concentration, and awareness. If you are in an energy slump, you'll probably just fall asleep.

But time, of course, is the crucial factor. When it comes to energy, it doesn't matter if you are a morning person if you already get up before dawn and immediately launch into an award-winning effort to get everyone in your family, including yourself, dispatched to their proper locations before school buses and carpools leave, meetings begin, and time clocks hit their designated hours.

If your only possible free time is your lunch hour or that precious interval between when the kids are asleep and when you collapse in bed, you'll probably find that evening is your best meditation time. Ideally, of course, your energy peak and your free time coincide, but we recognize it isn't a perfect world.

Whatever time works, pick a time and stick to it whenever possible. Keep that time sacred and instruct the people who live with you to respect your meditation time. Turn on the answering machine, go to your meditation space leaving all other responsibilities behind, and be at peace.

Start Slow

Now you've probably got a pretty clear idea of what your priorities are for your meditation practice, when to do it, where to do it, even how to do it. Can I finally get started? you may be pleading to the pages of this book. All right, all right, let's do it! But don't expect us to rush into anything. Indeed, rushing is contrary to the very nature of meditation. Remember the fable of the tortoise and the hare? Slow and steady will get you there.

When you first sit down (or lie down or stand up or whatever form you are trying), make your goal a good five minutes of meditation. For first-timers, this may be the longest five minutes you've ever experienced! Your nose might itch, your muscles might twitch, and you'll probably run down every to-do list on your agenda before you remember to remind yourself that you are meditating. Don't worry. That's usually how it is at first. It will get better.

Stick with five-minute sessions for three days, then move up to seven minutes the next day, eight minutes the following day, nine minutes the next day, then on the seventh day, 10 minutes. Stick with 10-minute sessions for one week, then move up to 15 for a week, then 20 minutes.

Twenty minutes twice per day is the recommended meditation schedule according to many instructors, but if you can only manage it once, that's great. In one month, you're there! If you can eventually work up to 30, 45, or even 60 minutes, that's great, too. Eventually, the goal is to be able to maintain a mindful, meditative state all the time,

Suggested schedule for beginners:

- ✓ Day two   5 minutes
- ✓ Day three   5 minutes
- ✓ Day four   7 minutes
- ✓ Day five   8 minutes
- ✓ Day six   9 minutes
- ✓ Day seven   10 minutes
- ✓ Week two   10 minutes
- ✓ Week three   15 minutes
- ✓ Week four   20 minutes

To keep track of the time, set a timer. If you're looking at a clock every minute or so, not only will the time seem interminable, but the clock will keep you from concentrating on your point of focus, and time will become too high a priority in your awareness. With a timer (a simple kitchen timer or egg timer with a bell will do), you can forget about the time until you hear the signal. Try to use a timer with a gentle ring and without a loud tick, tick, tick.

Be Diligent

Diligence is another important quality to cultivate when beginning a meditation practice. Without perseverance and discipline, you'll soon give up. Maybe your parents used to tell you that nothing worth having comes easily. That's usually true, and it's true here, too. Meditation takes time to yield its benefits.

In many ways, our modern society is an undisciplined one. We don't want to wait for anything. We have fast food. We have drive-thru banks, dry-cleaners, pharmacies, even drive-thru quick shops! (As if quick shops aren't quick enough.) We want everything that might be a little tedious done for us. We're glad to pay money for it, but what spiritual price are we paying as we shell out the big bucks? Sometimes it may seem like no one wants to work for anything anymore. It's easier to buy a lottery ticket than earn your own living. (But not easier to win!)

But you can change all that, at least for yourself. (And perhaps the world can change, too, slowly, person by person.) One step at a time, one aspect of your life at a time, cultivate discipline. Be diligent about the very task of living. Meditation can be the groundwork of that diligence. You can do it! You can change your life, one Om at a time.

A Little Progress on a Long Road to Samadhi

The road to enlightenment—whatever enlightenment means to you—is a long one, fraught with obstacles. But you can find your bliss, little by little. Although meditation won't result in immediate, dramatic benefits, it does yield tiny treasures along the way. One day, you may suddenly realize that your work demands don't get to you the way they used to. Or your spouse's annoying little habits aren't so annoying. Maybe you find you are seeing a brilliant sunset or a snowy forest or a bed of pink tulips for the very first time, and the sight fills you with sudden joy.

Maybe you will look in the mirror one day and will, quite unexpectedly, love what you see, and it will have nothing to do with your external appearance. Maybe your movements will develop more grace, your speech will become more relaxed, or your demeanor will suddenly radiate composure. Maybe one month, day by day, your life will look more and more like a garden every day. Then you'll see how worthwhile a daily meditation practice can be.

Leave Your Pride on the Doorstep

In this competitive world, the idea of pouring your time and energy into something that has nothing to do with competition, besting anyone, or winning may seem a little hard to swallow. But meditation isn't about being the best, but only about learning to be the best that you can be. Can you imagine a competitive attitude applied to meditation?

Check me out I'm way more relaxed than you'll ever be! Ha! I attained enlightenment first! Pretty ridiculous, huh! The whole point of meditation is to remove stress-inducing mentalities and ideally, to come to the realization we are all one. And if we are all one, then competition is pointless.

If you are naturally competitive, let your nature help your personal journey rather than hinder it. Meditation on a regular basis will soften the winner/loser aspects of competition. You may find your focus shifts to finding win/win situations for everyone! Indeed, everyone is a winner in meditation, a highly personal journey of self-discovery.

Going the Distance

Meditation is a journey, just like life. It's a long journey, but a rewarding journey. Be ready to persevere and be patient. Some stretches on this road go on for miles, like a trip across the desert. Yet, even the desert, though it looks dry and brown at first glance, reveals its wonders when you really concentrate on the view.

Of course, no journey begins until you take that first step, so when you're ready (and you are), sit down, take a deep breath, and begin. To borrow a slogan from a company that thrives on appareling competitive bodies, "Just do it."

Make meditation a part of your lifestyle, of who you are.

Chapter 9: Daily Meditation Worksheets

Incorporating meditation techniques into your daily routine takes practice and consistency. One way to ensure this happens is to set up a daily or weekly plan of meditation activities to help keep you on track. You may use the sample template below and fill in the mediation exercises or techniques you prefer for each day of the week. On the last column, you can write down your feedback on how the meditation exercise made you feel, how it benefited you, how you felt before and after the exercise, and any other comments relevant to your experience. For a more detailed list on how to properly perform the following exercises, you may check out each meditation task below.

DAY	MEDITATION EXERCISE	FEEDBACK
Monday	Mindfulness Meditation	
Tuesday	Body Scan	
Wednesday	Mindful Eating	
Thursday	Five Senses Exercise	
Friday	Progressive Muscle Relaxation	
Saturday	Diaphragmatic Breathing	
Sunday	Visualization	

Mindfulness Meditation

First, you will need to find a place where you can sit quietly and remain undisturbed for a few moments.

You may use a timer and set it to 10 minutes. You may also start at a much lesser timeframe such as 5 minutes and progress from there. The length of time you spend on mindfulness meditation shouldn't really matter at first.

As you notice your breathing, bring yourself to the present moment. With each breath that enters and exits your body, pay close attention. Pretty soon, you will find yourself starting to pull out of the present moment by wandering off with different thoughts in your mind. When this happens, do not fret –just let it be. Instead, take notice on these thoughts and feelings you have as if you are just an outsider to your own thoughts, while watching the workings behind your brain. Take notes and allow yourself to return to your breathing.

It is common to find yourself being bored or even frustrated. Your mind might start to wander off towards making plans for the days ahead, or to that pending work email. Take notice of these things and where your thoughts are going.

When you can, try to shift your focus back to your breathing. Continue this process until your timer is up, or when you are finally ready to finish.

Body Scan Meditation

Doing a body scan meditation is a great way to pay close attention to your physical sensations you may feel throughout your body. The goal is to make your body relax progressively. It generally doesn't matter how long you do it in practice, just as long as you do it slowly.

Start by paying attention to the sensations of your feet. Notice these sensations such as the coolness or warmth, pain or pressure, or even just the breeze moving through and over your skin. Then, slowly move up your attention to from your feet up to each body part, finally ending with your head. Spend some time on these body parts, while noticing the sensations they bring.

After you scan through your body, move the opposite way. Start to move back down, through each of your body part that you've just went through, up until the point where you reach your feet again.

While doing this exercise, it is important to just move slowly and to pay attention, instead of rushing the whole process without paying close enough attention to the activity.

Mindful Eating

This activity can easily be done with a myriad of different food choices. Preferably, the food should be something you can hold in your hand without it getting messy. Even something small and simple like a sunflower seed or a raisin would work for this exercise.

Even before picking up the food of your choice, notice what it looks like on the table in front of you. Pay attention to its color, its size, or even how the light reflects from its surface.

Next, pick up the food. Feel it against your palm or your skin and notice how much it weighs, the textures, and so on. Roll the object in your hand, in between your fingers, on your palm, and feel its texture. Determine how smooth or rough it is, how firm or soft, if there is any slickness, or any other properties it may have. Hold the food up to your nose and pay close attention to its smell.

Next, place the food in your mouth, on your tongue, but don't eat it just yet. Pay attention to the feel of it inside your mouth. Is the texture similar to the feel on your hand? What does it taste like? Roll the food around your mouth and pay attention to the sensations you are feeling.

Next, begin to chew your food. Notice how easily or how difficult it is to sink your teeth into it. As you bite and chew on it, notice its texture and feel. Pay close attention to the different flavor profiles you are discovering while chewing. Do the flavors burst out of it in waves, or are they flavors more subdued in nature and only come over time? Notice how these flavors come together and spread all across your tongue. Does your tongue feel hot or cold? Does your mouth immediately fill with saliva after taking a bite of the food? Continue to chew your food, paying attention to as many sensations as you can. Finally, finish your food while still focusing on these different textures and experiences, up until your last swallow.

Five Senses Exercise

If you want a quick exercise that can help you ground yourself in the present moment, then this Five Senses meditation exercise is the perfect tool for you. The main goal is to simply notice something you are currently experiencing through each of your senses.

Look around your surroundings and notice at least 5 things you haven't noticed before. What are 5 things your eyes can see? It can be the lighting reflecting on the surface of the wall, a small trinket or decorative piece at the edge of the room, or maybe the wallpaper pattern. Pay attention to these and take them all in.

As you are standing or sitting down, notice the sensations on your feet. What are 4 things you can feel? Is it the smoothness or the roughness of the ground beneath your feet? Or maybe there is pressure from the shirt resting on your shoulders. Or maybe it is the temperature of your body and of your skin, one that feels either hot or cold to you. Next, pick up a near object and notice its texture.

The next thing you will need to do is to pay attention to the sounds around you. What are 3 things you can hear? Take notice of all the background sounds you have been filtering out such as the chirping of birds outside your window, or the humming of the air conditioner, or even the sound of passing cars on the street.

Next is to notice the things that you smell. What are 2 things you can clearly smell? Is it the subtle fragrance of flowers outside, or the roasted aroma of your freshly brewed cup of coffee? It doesn't really have to be a pleasant smell – you may even notice the smell of garbage outside or the sewer.

What is 1 thing you can taste? Have a sip of a drink, or pop a treat into your mouth. Eat a snack if you must, but the most important thing is to really just notice how your mouth takes in the taste and the sensations that go along with it. You may even "taste" the air if you don't have any food nearby.

These numbers for determining how many things you need to feel are just samples – feel free to add more items to each sense. Also, this is an activity that can easily be done even when you are doing chores or doing an activity such as listening to music, going for a walk, washing the dishes, or walking your way to work. Whatever it is you're doing at the present moment; the important thing is to become fully aware of everything that happens around you as you are doing these things. This self-awareness with provide you better insight into the world of meditation and help you become a more focused, attentive individual.

Progressive Muscle Relaxation

Assume a comfortable position, whether it is sitting, lying down, or simply standing up.

Next, try to tense each of the muscles in your body for about 5 seconds. Then get ready for progressively relaxing them.

Start by taking a few deep breaths from the abdomen. With each muscle group, try to tense, hold, and relax, while working your way up or down your body.

Try and notice the contrast between a tensed state and a relaxed state inhaling as you tense the muscle and exhaling as you relax and try to let go of each muscle.

With consistency in practice, you can do a variation of this technique wherein whole muscle groups are tensed and relaxed at the same time.

This technique reduces any physiological tension caused by thoughts that have the tendency to provoke anxiety in a person.

Diaphragmatic Breathing

On a supportive surface, lie down on your back.

With a pillow, support your head while bending your knees. You may also opt to place a support pillow below your knees.

Place one hand below your rib cage, and another hand on your chest.

Breathe in deeply and slowly through your nose so you can feel the hand on your stomach slowly rising.

Allow the muscles in your stomach to tense up as they begin to tighten when you exhale through your lips.

Repeat this breathing meditation technique for about 5-10 minutes, for at least 3-4 times a day is possible. This type of deep breathing is excellent for relieving stress and anxiety, as shallow breathing can contribute to these restless feelings. Diaphragmatic breathing makes us aware of abdominal breathing which allows your respiratory system to function properly.

Visualization

Begin by closing your eyes and taking your mind to a relaxing and peaceful place. This may be your favorite beach or park, or just a general picture of your ideal place that soothes and calms your mind and soul.

Let your imagination wander through this place, and try to feel and see everything that this place has to offer. Feel the warmth of the sun on your skin, or the coolness of the breeze, the sound of the ocean waves, the smell of the crisp mountain air, or the greenness of the pine trees. Make your visualization as detailed as possible.

If you find your thoughts wandering, acknowledge this and go back to breathing in order to dismiss them. Visualization is a great way to practice seeing things with all of your senses. It is a wonderful way to allow your mind to go on a mini-vacation, and thereby relax the body, clam the mind, and clear away any clutter or toxic thought of the day.

Relaxing Breathing

This is a straightforward breathing technique that uses 4-7-8 breathing exercise. It involves counting your breath while counting to 4, then holding the breath up to the count of 7, then exhaling up to the count of 8.

To start, sit upright with your spine and back straight and make sure to relax your shoulders.

Put the tip of your tongue against the base of the tissue just behind the upper front of your teeth, making sure to keep your tongue in place as you perform the breathing exercise.

Through your nose, inhale up to a count of 4.

Hold your breath for about 7 seconds.

Next, exhale through your mouth for at least 8 seconds. This inhale-hold-exhale exchange is considered one cycle of breath, and you may choose to repeat this for 3 or 4 times more.

This technique is considered to be a natural tranquilizer for your nervous system. You may choose to perform this when you feel stress is coming on.

Counting Breathing

Start by finding a comfortable position for you to exercise, keeping your back straight and your spine aligned.

With your eyes closed, take a few deep breaths in and out and breathe naturally.

When you inhale, mentally count to one and then slowly exhale.

As you exhale, do so slowly. Then take another inhalation and count to two this time.

Repeat this breathing cycle until to feel like doing it, or until you reach the count you are aiming for. Strive for at least a ten-minute breathing practice.

Meditation to Improve Concentration

Also called focused meditation, this is a great way to improve your focus and concentration.

To start, find an object to focus on. If you prefer to hold the object, you may do so.

Start by closing your eyes and focusing your attention on your breath, breathing slowly and deeply.

Next, begin to focus on your object. You may study the object for a brief moment and look at it closely, noticing the little details. Next, gently close your eyes again.

If you are picturing an object and it is not being held out in front of you, start thinking about what you can recall about the item. If you are inside, you can also just focus on any item that's in the room, such as a lamp, a book, a shelf, or a decorative piece.

Imagine this object in every little detail, taking note of its color, its texture, its shape, size, and so on.

As you close your eyes, try to recall every little detail of this object in your mind's eye and see how powerful your perception of this object is. Even the minute details of that tiniest crack or littlest bump can be used as part of your meditation process. With more practice, it will be easier for you to recall all of these little details, which can help sharpen your focus.

Gratitude Meditation

This type of meditation is where you get the chance to reflect on all the gifts in your life. While it may seem like a simple practice, it can produce significant results.

Start by focusing your attention on the things you feel grateful for, such as your family, your career, your house, etc. This helps put your mind to a safe, welcoming space and help you focus on the positive and shy away from the negative.

Slowly, you may begin to feel positive emotions such as gratitude, kindness, loving, and compassion. Your awareness broadens and your creativity and problem-solving capacities begin to expand.

For a shorter and quicker version of this type of meditation, you can start by listing about 5-7 things you feel grateful for like a warm home, a soft blanket, a loving spouse, a caring friend, or even a good job or financial security.

Stillness Meditation

This is a great meditation technique that can be taught to students of meditation. It brings the focus on stillness, and finding peace in it.

First, find a place to sit still and while listening to soothing music that will be put on play. Listen to this without moving.

Have the light dimmed down and set a timer for about 3-5 minutes.

The goal of this meditation challenge is to simply sit with your eyes closed without moving or fidgeting too much.

Once the timer goes off, open your eyes and stretch it out. You may repeat the cycle with a more extended time frame.

Breathing Buddy Meditation

This breathing meditation method involves the use of a stuffed animal. You can choose any stuffed item as you wish.

Next, set a timer for about 3-5 minutes and place the stuffed toy on your belly as you rest.

If at any point, the stuffed animal falls, put it back on and keep breathing. The main goal or objective is to focus on your breathing while balancing the object for as long as you can.

Worksheet 1: How to Quiet Your Mind in the Midst of Chaos

- ✓ Step 1: Focus on your breathing. Pay attention to how you are breathing. Listen to what your breathing says to you and how it makes you feel. You might be feeling agitated, or calm, or energized and that's okay. The important thing is awareness towards these feelings. Write down these emotions as you continue to focus on your breathing.

- ✓ Step 2: Develop a sense of gratitude. There are surely a lot of things to be grateful for in everyday, and this is the perfect time for you to list these all down. Include your health, your family, your friendships, all other relationships, financial security, abundance, etc.

- ✓ Step 3: Set up your intention for the day. This next step will have you set up your intention for the rest of the day. It can be anything from setting the intention to be present at all times or to remain calm despite a very challenging situation. Or it can be as simple as intending to feel grounded. List down all your intentions for the day, regardless of how little or how many they are.

- ✓ Step 4: Make the decision to let go. This is when you delve deeper into yourself in order to separate those which no longer serve you and those which actually do. Decide to let these go. For example, you don't have to feel liked by everyone, so you can let go of this need to be perfect at all times. Ask yourself what are the things worth letting go of?

Worksheet 2: STOP Technique

- ✓ Anytime you feel anxious or worried, this is a wonderful technique to practice.

- ✓ Stop – Whatever it is you are doing, stop and put things down if only for a moment.

- ✓ Take – Take 2-3 nice deep breaths and strive to breathe all the way into your lower belly.

- ✓ Observe – Observe your emotions and how you are feeling. Note what are the thoughts, feelings, or emotions are running through your mind and come to terms with the fact that these are not permanent. These feelings are fleeting and they easily come and go as they please. Even the simple act of putting a name to these emotions can reduce your fear of how you are handling situations in your stressful and busy life.

- ✓ Proceed – Proceed with something that can help you out or support you in the moment. It can be calling a friend to chat over coffee, or talking to your partner.

Worksheet 3: Letting Go of Your Story

- ✓ Find a quiet place where you can be comfortable to remain undisturbed for a period of time.

- ✓ Begin by asking yourself the stories you believe about yourself and about how they might be holding back from being happy or successful. Then ask yourself what you truly want.

- ✓ Next, think about how you introduce yourself to others or what you tell others about yourself.

- ✓ Once you have identified this, notice how your body reacts to these feelings when you tell your own story.

- ✓ Notice the thoughts that begin to appear when you believe and listen to this story of yours.

- ✓ Next, ask yourself if this story is an accurate depiction of yourself and who created this story for yourself.

- ✓ Begin to imagine what it would feel like if you never actually believed this story and see how it feels like to let go if the associated feelings that come with it.

- ✓ Observe how you would feel if you let this story go.

- ✓ Ask yourself what you would do differently if you did not believe this story.

- ✓ As you go about the rest of your day, ask yourself what is the story you are trying to hold on to, and what might still be holding you back.
- ✓ When letting go of your story, practice patience. Learn to adapt self-compassion and love.

Chapter 10: Taking the Edginess Off in the Modern Day

First you have to bring the power of penetrating insight to bear on your habitual patterns and stories; otherwise, healthier perspectives and patterns can't take root, and you just keep running in the same old grooves.

Seeing beyond your story to who you really are

Even though you may become aware of your story, gain some distance from it, and begin to alter it in certain fundamental ways, you may still identify with it until you can catch a glimpse of who you really are, beyond your story.

Such glimpses can take a number of different forms. Perhaps you have unexpected moments of peace or tranquility, when your thoughts settle down or even stop entirely and a sweet silence permeates your mind. Or you may experience a flood of unconditional love that momentarily opens your heart wide and gives you a brief glimpse of the oneness beyond all apparent separation.

Or maybe you have a sudden intuition of your inherent interconnectedness with all beings or a sense of being in the presence of something far vaster than yourself. Whatever the insight that lifts you beyond your story, it can irrevocably alter who you take yourself to be. Never again can you fully believe you're merely the limited personality your mind insists you are.

 I can still remember how fresh and clear everything appeared after my first meditation retreat the colors so vivid, people's faces so radiant — even though I'd spent five days doing nothing but struggling to count my breaths from one to ten without losing my way. I felt as though a bandage had been ripped from my eyes and I could see things clearly for the first time.

Everything I encountered seemed to radiate being, and I knew as never before that I belonged on this Earth. Of course, the intensity faded after a few days, but I never forgot that first glimpse of clear seeing, free from the perceptual filters I'd been carrying around for a lifetime.

Freeing yourself from your story

When you've caught a glimpse of who you really are, beyond your mind (and even your body), you can keep reconnecting with this deeper level of being in your meditations and in your everyday life as well. To resurrect the metaphor of the lake, you can dive down to the bottom again and again because you know what it looks like and how to find it.

 Even though your story may continue to play on the video screen of your brain, you can develop the capacity to disengage from it or even disidentify from it entirely. As a friend of mine put it, you come to realize that the personality is a case of mistaken identity and who you are is the vast expanse of being itself, in which your personal thoughts and feelings arise and pass away.

Such a profound realization may take years of meditation to achieve, yet it's always available to you, no matter how long you've meditated indeed, whether you've ever meditated at all! Many people report laughing uproariously.

Benefit of Meditation

Mindfulness meditation is a holistic tool for growth and self awareness. It benefits the mind, body, and soul as a whole, however for this papers purpose I will separate the components into the benefits related to psychological, philosophical, and spiritual elements of the human being. These will be based on the literature pertaining to mindfulness meditation specifically and what has been discussed in a variety of research studies.

Meditation Is a Great Stressbuster

It isn't easy to get through the day without hearing something about stress in the modern world. Television shows, magazine articles, and books tell us that we are a stressed-out society. They tell us what causes our stress, they tell us why stress is bad, and they give us all kinds of suggestions about what we should be doing to relieve our stress.

In fact, the barrage of stress-talk out there is pretty darned stressful!

But it's true that we are a stressed-out society. Stress helps to define the character of the modern world, and it can even be helpful when you need to get a job done fast or when you need to handle an emergency. In fact, stress is incredibly beneficial in times of crisis. The problem is, long-term stress is dangerous and damaging to your health.

The stress/illness link is a hard one to pinpoint because stress causes such a wide variety of symptoms and has different manifestations in different people, but stress is most directly associated with the adrenal glands. These glands secrete hormones in reaction to situations or conditions, whether physical or psychological, that cause tension or strain to the body and/or the mind.

One of the best known of these hormones is adrenaline, which heightens our senses and reflexes, preparing us for action to handle the stress. Another is cortisol, a hormone that has been shown in many studies to be elevated in times of stress and decreased by relaxation activities like meditation and massage. Some of the physical symptoms of stress caused by the secretion of stress hormones are:

- ✓ Elevated blood pressure
- ✓ Muscle contraction
- ✓ The movement of blood toward the muscles and nervous system and away from the digestive organs
- ✓ Fluid retention in the kidneys
- ✓ Increased levels of chemicals responsible for coagulating blood

- ✓ The break-down of certain proteins to form glucose, which acts as an anti-inflammatory

These conditions are useful in emergencies. For example, muscles prepare for defensive or offensive action. Fluid is retained in the kidneys and the blood becomes ready to coagulate quickly in case of bleeding. The body readies itself to fight inflammation and infection. But bodies aren't meant to function under these conditions for long periods of time. Eventually, your body will break down.

Of course, stress is inevitable in our culture and the best way to handle it is to avoid what stress you can, but also to prepare your mind and body to handle the necessary stress. A healthy diet will help and so will exercise. But in this particular world at this particular time, most of us don't have to face wild animals, hunting and digging for our own food, and the physical drama of a nomadic existence. Our stresses are mainly mental. How many times a day do you clench your fists, your face, or your mind and think, What am I going to do about this?

That's why meditation is so crucial for handling stress, right now, today, in your life. Needless to say, any practice Many studies have demonstrated the beneficial effects of meditation (some studies included other stress-relief techniques and/or lifestyle changes like yoga practice), which include:

- ✓ Fewer doctor visits
- ✓ Lower cholesterol levels
- ✓ Lower blood pressure levels

- ✓ Less heart disease
- ✓ Reversal of arteriosclerosis (hardened arteries)
- ✓ Reduced angina (chest pain)
- ✓ Lower levels of stress hormones in the blood
- ✓ Altered brain wave patterns reflective of a calmer state
- ✓ Fewer accidents and less absenteeism at work
- ✓ Less depression
- ✓ Increased confidence, awareness, and general health

Meditation Promotes Mind-Body Fitness

We can hardly talk about mental fitness without bringing physical fitness into the conversation. Really, fitness applies to your whole self, physical and mental, so anything that helps one aspect will help the other.

For example, meditation helps you have a calmer, more tranquil mind that can better handle stress. It also reduces stress in your body, so your body is able to maintain a healthy state more effectively. A healthy body feels good, and feeling good makes you feel even better about yourself and your life. When you feel good, you want to maintain the feeling. When you feel good about yourself, you want to take care of yourself. Exercise is one of the best ways to take care of yourself and can help to increase and maintain that feeling of health and well-being.

Exercise has also been shown to improve the mental state, from a general mood lift to lessening the symptoms of severe depression. A positive mental state is ideal for meditation, and meditation can make the most of a positive mental state. See how it's all connected?

Mind-body fitness is the ultimate fitness goal, and the only true complete approach. Meditation, then, should be as integral to your fitness program as your daily run in the park, your weightlifting sessions, or your Hatha Yoga class.

Meditation Is Healing Power

But meditation is more than stress relief, fitness ally, and preventive medicine. Meditation can help when injury or illness is already in the picture. Studies have shown how meditation and similar relaxation techniques can reverse certain aspects of heart disease. Meditation is also used with sometimes-dramatic effectiveness in pain clinics, helping patients to deal with pain more effectively, and in some cases, to reduce or eliminate pain.

Meditation comes in many forms, and some forms may be more effective than others for particular health problems, but the overall benefits are undeniable. The mind is a powerful ally in healing the body, and meditation keeps the mind primed.

It also keeps the mind-body balanced. It's easy to become imbalanced when life gets busywe neglect our health maintenance routines, become increasingly stressed, and suddenly lose perspective. Have you ever exploded over something clearly not worth a major episode, such as a misplaced pen or a coffee spill? Maybe a headache puts you out of commission for the rest of the day because it becomes the proverbial straw that broke the camel's back.

Forget it! you might cry, throwing up your hands. I'm going home to bed! Stress throws us out of balance because it alters our body systems away from their normal operating conditions, or homeostasis.

To compensate, we often take medications, which may further imbalance our homeostasis (although in some cases, of course, medication can help to restore an imbalance). For some conditions, including general stress and many chronic health problems, meditation is a better and more effective way to restore homeostasis than aspirin, antacids, or caffeine pills.

Meditation reminds your body of how it is supposed to be by clearing out the distractions and stressors lingering in your busy brain. Meditation can help the body to get back on track and reclaim its healing power. And when you finally start to heal, you'll start feeling really, really good.

Love Thy Mind, Love Thy Body, Love Thyself

One of meditation's most important benefits may be the effect it has on your self-concept. Sure, you like yourself.

You're okay. But you probably have a long list of your own glaring imperfections, even if most or all of them are things no one would notice but you. Most people are fairly self-critical, and self-examination is good. You can learn from your mistakes if you study yourself and use what you observe to continually evolve. But self-flagellation isn't good. If you can't give yourself a break, why should anyone else?

Meditation takes away all that petty, nit-picky self-loathing. Depending on your philosophy, meditation helps you to love yourself by showing you who you really are inside, by teaching you that you are simply one individual expression of nature, or by empowering you to know and control your own mind-body (and not become so attached to your concept of it).

Moving toward any of these ideas will help you learn to love your mind, love your body, and meet your mind-body (perhaps for the first time). Most important, meditation can teach you to love yourself - your whole self.

So, even if you've always thought meditation sounded a little weird, you are probably willing to admit the benefits sound compelling. What have you got to lose? Twenty minutes? Chances are, it will eventually become the best 20 minutes of your day.

Chapter 11: Making Meditation a Daily Habit

Meditation Techniques for Busy People

Meditation is very important for our busy lives, but it can be quite a challenge to always find ways to incorporate it into your daily life. We want to meditate in order to slow down our fast-paced lifestyle, yet when we do make time for meditation, our mind goes flying out towards our work, courses, or other trivial matters, just as easily as when we lose ourselves while watching our favorite soaps or when we scroll through social media sites.

In this modern world of constant stimulation, meditation seems very difficult to perform. Many people believe meditation is all about emptying the mind. Instead, it teaches one to focus on one thing at a time. Meditation doesn't fail to work when the mind wanders. Instead, our mind does what it can to put itself back on track in meditation. Many people may find meditation very boring to do initially. This is because all you need to do is close your eyes and count breaths, and as soon as this happens to the untrained minds, you start making "to-do" lists and start worrying about getting those items checked off from the list. But to give it time, time enough to know and practice it wholly, can be very beneficial.

There are a lot of reasons why meditation is hard for busy people. One of these reasons include the fact we tend to wear too many hats all at once. We are busy juggling our careers, children, homes, and other social responsibilities. These days, we hardly ever have one role to play. Mothers are also career women, fathers are also great sons, and so forth.

But meditation doesn't require hours of our time in a day. in fact, even just 5 minutes to stop and breathe can already count as your initial workout towards meditation. The important thing is to start small and to start slowly. Once you feel ready to level up, increase your meditation time form 5 minutes to 8 minutes. Then, progress to 10 minutes, then 15, then 20, and so on.

You can also actually find time to meditate while doing chores such as cleaning, eating, walking, or even while working. Incorporate meditation techniques into your daily routine tasks, and soon you will notice you can save your time with doing just regular meditation.

Another issue that prevents most people from doing meditation is that they find it too boring. Let's face it, when we do get free time from our busy schedules, we like to indulge in things we seldom find time to do, things we actually enjoy. These can range from doing sports, to hobbies such as crafting, or reading, or even going on a small holiday.

But learning how to quiet your mind also has its own perks, and these mostly serve to further relax and refresh your already too tired mind and body. if you find your mind wandering towards work or other tasks and plans during your meditation, simply bring it back to breathing.

Being mindful as to when you do start wandering means that you are actually successful in observing your mind. To prevent yourself from overthinking, allow yourself to plan or think about these important things for only a certain period of time. After getting the thinking out of these things, you can then actually focus on practicing your meditation mindfully.

While many people acknowledge the importance of meditation, not everyone knows how to get started. It is more than just reading meditation books, or buying CDs of classical music, or taking classes. The first step is to actually start small and improvise your timing. It needs a few days, weeks, or even months to get used to. But progress can never happen if you don't take that crucial first step. With consistency in application, practice makes progress.

Meditation while Walking

Whether you are walking your dog, taking a long leisurely hike, or walking fast to catch your bus, you can incorporate meditation at all times. The key is to pay attention to one thing at a time, like how your feet feels when they touch the ground, or observing the color of the trees around you, or just listening and observing the sound the cicadas of the night make. Whenever you feel your mind wandering, just take it back to your focused breathing. Breathing meditation can be practiced anytime and anywhere you go. It can significantly reduce stress and help you connect to nature.

Red Light Meditation

If you make the commute by driving your car to work, you can perform this type of meditation known as red light meditation. If you have just stopped at the traffic signal, turn your car radio or stereo off, then take a few deep, long breaths, keeping your eyes open. Once your mind goes off, get back to breathing. This breathing meditation can help you reduce stress and refresh your overworked mind.

Meditation while Drinking/Eating

Whenever you eat your meals, try to focus on the different textures, flavors, and the feel of the food or drinks you are enjoying. Paying close attention to these little things can help you improve your focus while ensuring you are thoroughly enjoying the moment of being able to satisfy your hunger and thirst. In turn, this will help you gain a deeper appreciation towards every bit of the food you eat and drink.

Meditation while Cycling or Running

While running or riding your bike, it is very common to keep your earphones at bay to help you enjoy the activity. But in order to inject meditation, keep these earphones away and tune in to the sensation of the activity you are doing. Feel the wind on your face, feel the force of your limbs that are strong enough to carry you from one place to another, the muscles that work in order to help you run or cycle, or feel the ground under your feet. Avoid jumping from focusing on one sensation to another in order to keep your meditation focus at its best.

Meditation while Waiting in Queue

It can't be helped – we will always find ourselves in a queue one way or another. It can be boring yes, but why not make full use of it? If you are in a queue, just explore your surroundings and consider your breathing. Do some inner observations and self-awareness until your turn is called or until you get your turn?

Do you feel hot or cold? Are your feet in pain from all the standing? Pay attention to these little sensations in your body but make sure not to judge them. if you are in the checkout line at the grocery store, refrain from judging others only because their shopping baskets contain very little items as compared to yours or to others. Simply notice and observe your surroundings without any judgement.

Task-based Meditation

Mindfulness meditation can be incorporated in daily life. whether you are folding the laundry, brushing your teeth, taking a shower, washing the dishes, or just washing your hands, you can perform mini meditations. This can easily be done by simply focusing on the experience of whatever it is you are doing and trying to keep your mind from thinking about anything else. By trying to focus on what's happening, you will be pulling your mind out of the ocean of thoughts that bombard your mind at all times of the day.

Chapter 12: The Obstacles and how to Best Prepare Yourself

The sad truth is while most of us are aware of the benefits of meditation, very few of us actually have a regular meditation practice. There are a lot of obstacles to overcome in order to incorporate meditation into our daily lives. I overcame those obstacles and have been meditating daily for two years, as well as meditating periodically throughout the day! Through meditation I have experienced more peace and joy in my life, I've become less reactive and less stressed and I have more energy and creativity! And I know you can experience these benefits as well!

Not having enough time

 The biggest obstacle people face in developing a regular meditation practice is TIME. We don't have enough time to meditate! (Interestingly enough this wasn't just an "American" phenomenon. People from all across the globe mentioned they didn't have enough time to meditate).

 Yet there are 4 simple ways to incorporate meditation into your life without taking ANY time out of your current schedule!

First, I invite you to convert your waiting time into meditating time.

The average person waits 45-60 minutes a day. We wait for appointments, we wait in traffic, we wait in line at the grocery store and we wait on hold on the phone. Yet those precious "waiting times" can be converted into meditating times.

So next time you are waiting for an appointment, take a moment to notice your breath. Or next time you are waiting in line at the grocery store, take a moment to smile from the inside.

Second, have a daily activity be your meditation. You can incorporate meditation into any of these daily activities:

- ✓ Brushing your teeth
- ✓ Emptying the dishwasher
- ✓ Showering
- ✓ Eating
- ✓ Walking
- ✓ Folding laundry, ironing

As you brush your teeth, notice your breath. Or notice the aliveness in your hands and mouth. As you empty the dishwasher, feel the aliveness in your hand as you put each dish away.

Third, have your dog or cat be your meditation! Have you ever noticed when walking your dog how your dog is completely in the moment, taking in its' surroundings?

Well you can join your dog in this blissful state. When walking the dog notice the aliveness in your feet with each step. Notice the aliveness of the trees, birds, your surroundings. While petting the cat, notice the softness of the fur. Be completely present with your dog or cat!

Four, meditate while driving! Now, of course, do NOT close your eyes and meditate while driving. But you can be completely present while driving, with your eyes open. While driving, notice the aliveness in your hands as you touch the steering wheel. Or at a stop sign or in traffic, notice your breath.

These are simple ways you can incorporate meditation into your daily life without taking ANY time out of your current schedule. If we all did these simple things, we'd have a daily meditation practice!

Lack of Self-Discipline

The second biggest obstacle people face in incorporating meditation into their daily life is lack of self-discipline! Meditation takes discipline. I know many of us start out with great intentions to meditate daily or to exercise daily and we might do it for a couple of weeks, but then we lack the discipline necessary to continue.

That's why life coaches, personal trainers and other professions have been created! To hold us accountable and to keep us focused!

So if you lack self-discipline, find a meditation partner! Ask your spouse, partner, friend, coworker to join you in incorporating meditation into your daily life. Hold each other accountable.

Or even if you can't find someone that wants to meditate with you, tell your spouse/friend/partner/coworker of your intention to meditate daily and ask him/her to check in with you and ask you how you are doing. Just as an exercise partner is beneficial and productive, a meditation partner can be too!

Not having the right place or space to meditate

The third biggest obstacle people mentioned is NOT having the right place or space to meditate! This is a "perceived obstacle." You can literally meditate anywhere; while driving a car or walking through a crowded mall.

People often use not having a special place or specific area as an excuse to NOT meditate. If we continually wait for the right circumstances to meditate, we'll never meditate.

I give people a meditation assignment: to meditate in a public place! They can walk through the wall and notice people and places, while observing their breath or noticing the aliveness in their feet.

Falling Asleep

The fourth most common obstacle to meditation is falling asleep. And yet many meditation CD's say that it's okay if you fall asleep because you are still receiving the benefits of meditation...The only benefit you're receiving is a peaceful sleep! And yet, that is a benefit too! Meditation is awareness. It's being fully present in the moment. When you're asleep, you're asleep, not meditating.

Here are some tips if you fall asleep while meditating:

- ✓ Don't meditate at night before bed. So often many of us want to meditate daily, but we don't think about it until we are in bed or getting ready for bed and then we try to meditate. Of course we'll fall asleep.
- ✓ Try meditating in the morning or mid-day when you are alert.
- ✓ Meditate in small increments throughout the day. Again, notice your breath for a couple minutes while brushing your teeth or showering.

Too many distractions

The fifth most common complaint from people is that there are too many distractions to meditate. Yet distractions don't have to be distractions.

For example, during one of my meditations, my cat Vinnie came up to me and started meowing. He wouldn't stop either. He wanted my attention. Now to most people, this would be a distraction and a reason to stop meditating. Instead, I opened my eyes, sat down on the floor with him and petted him while noticing my breath. I incorporated my cat into my meditation. Instead of allowing him to become a distraction, he became my meditation!

If you are meditating and a distraction happens. Just notice it. Allow it to be. If it's something that needs your attention, tend to whatever needs to be done, while still observing your breath!

Not knowing how to meditate

So many people feel that they don't know how to meditate. We make meditation more complicated than it really is! Again, meditation is about being present in the moment. It's really about finding what works for you!

Again, you can incorporate meditation into your life without taking time out of your schedule. Your life can become a meditation. It is those moments throughout the day that we are fully present in the moment that matter. And through meditation, we discover the bliss of being what we are!

How to best Prepare Yourself for Meditation

Before starting any meditation technique, it is necessary to have a calm and quiet mind. It is only when the mind is free that real meditation can be experienced. There are exercises that you can do by yourself to help quieten the mind. You may try one or the other before you start your practice of meditation techniques. There is no one exercise known to work best. Each exercise would work differently from one meditator to another.

Although these exercises achieve the same results of a calm and quiet mind, they are different in the ways in which this state of mind is achieved. Meditation exercises include among others relaxation exercises, breathing exercises, concentration exercises, mantra exercises and visualization exercises.

What is Your Focus?

What you focus on is what you create. So the time before meditation spend time bringing your focus to think about your meditation time. What do you want for your meditation today? Is there a prayer in your heart for your meditation? Is there an issue in your life that needs attention, clarity, resolve? What do you want from meditating today?

Focusing in like this is preparing your mind and heart for a powerful start of your meditation. You are not wondering whereabouts unknown. You have an intention, a purpose, you are moving through your day with your eyes on your inner compass.

Create a Space Conducive for Going Within

It can support your meditation practice greatly to create a place that offers you inspiration, calm and peace the moment you enter it for meditation. You can dedicate a room to this purpose or a nice corner somewhere in your house. The more simple the decorations are the more it invites a feeling of calm and peace. Bring something to this space that gives you inspiration to go within. It can be a beautiful picture of nature, a picture of a saint or a master, anything that reminds you of the love and truth you are cherishing.

Tend also to the practical things you need. I always meditate with a box of Tissues, water bottle, hand towel and my journal. You can play music if you like and dimmed lighting or a candle really works nicely.

People that have created a space specifically for meditation tend to hold to their commitment to meditate 80% more of the time than people who do not have a dedicated space available.

Prepare Your Body

It is nice to be clean and free of any odours before going into meditation. They actually can be a distraction for yourself or others of you meditate in a group. Brush your teeth, put on fresh and loose fitting clothes. It is nice to have a clean feeling about you. Cleaning yourself in preparation can be like a cleansing, you cleanse yourself of all the 'muck' of the day.

Sitting Down versus Laying Down

Research has proven that laying down promotes us to go to sleep and thus is not really to be present in our meditation anymore. Meditation is about being awake, being clear. I recommend you sit up straight and comfortable enough so your body will not distract you during your meditations. The most asked question is if one needs to sit in the lotus position to get the most benefits from meditation.

My answer is this; Yes it is proven that when we sit up dead straight and have our legs crossed and our fingers in the mudrah position the kundalini energy in our spine can move about more freely and helps us to reach deeper states of consciousness when going within. But my experience is that many people have this happen by meditating in many different other positions too. I suggest it is better to sit up comfortably and be able to go deep then to try to sit in a lotus position and be distracted by discomfort of the body. So I suggest you find your own way with this.

Empty Your Mind

Meditation is NOT a way of making your mind quiet. It is a way of entering into the quiet that is already there - buried under the 50,000 thoughts the average person thinks every day.

A way to prepare yourself to have the mind be relatively 'empty' so you can focus within is to write down all the present thoughts you have, things you are trying to remember, things unresolves from the day perhaps. Just calmly sit and write all thoughts down until you mind feels relatively empty and it certainly is not trying to "hold or remember" any information or to dos.

Trying to stop your mind from thinking is like trying to stop a river from flowing with your bare hands... it's exhausting and almost impossible to accomplish!

When you learn how to meditate, you learn to step out of the river, and let your thoughts flow past you effortlessly.

When you learn to do this, you will find that your river of thoughts slows down all by itself. No effort is required.

Meditation is an act of letting go - not an act of shutting down.

Let Go of Expectations

It is important for you to let go of any expectation you might have about your meditation. Sometimes we desire to have an experience we had before again because it was so wonderful. This desire can stop the flow and be in the way of what wants to happen in meditation right now and we might not get the experience we needed to take our next step forward. Letting go of expectation help us to be more open to what is happening and that what wants to happen in response to our desire.

Focus On Your Reason to Meditate

Spiritual desire is to meditation what the sun is to human life; we need the sun to keep our life forces going, and we need spiritual desire to sustain our focus and endeavors in each second of meditation. Everything stems from your spiritual desire. You do not have to see at as spiritual desire if that does not resonate with you. You can see it as your motivation, your intention or you drive to improve and evolve. What ever you call it, this kind of desire is a feeling within, and it is what sustains your focus as you meditate.

So take some moment at the beginning of your meditation and reflect on your intent, the very reason why you are sitting down and going within. Focus on it and let yourself connect to feeling it. Let this feeling of spiritual desire carry you all the way in.

Chapter 13: The Future Of Meditation

Now that meditation has become so popular in the West, you may wonder how its influence will expand and evolve over the decades to come. Needless to say, no one really knows, but I'd be happy to offer some informed speculation, based on recent developments and cutting-edge research.

Some of the latest scientific studies use state-of-the-art technology to prove that regular meditation makes you happier, more empathic, and more resistant to disease. Coupled with earlier studies indicating a host of other health benefits, this growing body of research could lead to the mainstreaming of meditation in a number of important ways.

Take two meditations and call me in the morning

More and more doctors may prescribe regular sitting practice along with insulin, beta blockers, and blood-pressure medication for patients with serious illnesses like diabetes, heart disease, and hypertension. Indeed, many healthcare practitioners already do! If the research into meditation's benefits continues to yield such convincing results, HMOs and other medical organizations may ultimately require physicians to include it as standard practice for certain ailments.

Talking back to Prozac

Mindfulness meditation has no harmful side effects and permanently lifts the mood of those who practice it for just three months. Then why don't psychiatrists dispense it first to their depressed or anxious patients, before potentially dangerous mind-altering drugs? Beats me! In a few years, though, more and more shrinks may be counseling their patients to follow their breathing, as well as take their medication. So the book you hold in your hands may find its rightful place on psychiatrists' shelves, alongside the Diagnostic and Statistical Manual of Mental Disorders!

Spinning, stretching, and sitting

As the health benefits of meditation are more widely accepted and acknowledged, health clubs, spas, and resorts may increasingly include meditation classes and workshops alongside aerobics, spinning, weight-training, and hatha yoga. After all, meditation enhances your enjoyment of life at every level and what better time to enjoy life than on a vacation!

Beyond these more obvious applications for meditation, I anticipate that meditation will become a more pervasive presence on the cultural landscape. Perhaps you'll be able to access meditation courses on TV, hear celebrity meditators eager to talk about their practice, and find regular references to meditation on sitcoms and talk shows, in newspapers and magazines.

Some other, more visionary possibilities: meditation booths in public places, meditation classes in public schools, regular meditation breaks instead of coffee breaks in the workplace, meditation rooms next to board rooms in corporations — even meditation meetings beside prayer meetings in the halls of Congress!

And why not? Because meditation reduces stress and improves health without ideological baggage, it's primed to infiltrate our lives in unprecedented and unpredictable — new ways.

Conclusion

Meditation is one of the great eastern practices that has started to take hold in western culture. In fact, people all over the world are benefiting from it, both in mind and body. So, why isn't everyone meditating? It could be that not everyone knows of all the amazing benefits like increased relaxation, and decreased levels of anxiety and depression.

Meditation is unique for every person. While there are some classic experiences that can be common to many, meditation brings you the experiences you need to return to Source. There is no fast path. As stated below, meditation requires commitment. Without commitment there is no progress.

Along with commitment, discrimination is very important. This is where decisions to continue or abort a chosen path must be based on research and knowledge, coupled with your own experience. It is sometimes very easy to run away from something new (like meditation, sungazing, yoga, t'ai chi, new food programs, etc.) because things are uncomfortable in the short term, thereby denying ourselves of the ultimate long term benefits.

Then again, it's definitely not helpful to stick with something just because we don't want to admit to ourselves that we made a mistake in going down a particular path. There is a fine line to walk and we must constantly choose and reevaluate our choices in light of our knowledge and experience.

The relaxation response from meditation surely yields a lot of healthful and positive benefits for the overall well-being of a person. It may seem intimidating and time consuming to do, but with consistency and discipline, you will eventually find it easy to incorporate into your daily activities. It doesn't have to be perfect, because the goal of meditation is for you to keep in tune with your inner self. With countless benefits that can help you rewire and balance your overall lifestyle; it is a worthy undertaking.

-- Dane Krauss

Dear Reader,

Thanks for exploring this book with me. Now that you know what meditation is all about…

…why not take one step further and develop a photographic memory?

You'll love the other book on the improvement of the mind, because it complements this one.

Get it now.

Thanks,

Dane

P.S. Reviews are like giving a warm hug to your favorite author. We love hugs.

https://www.amazon.com/dp/B083LC1KRN

Check Out Other Books

https://www.amazon.com/dp/B07K3CJ562

https://www.amazon.com/dp/B07KMBX8RF

https://www.amazon.com/dp/B0856SZJXT

https://www.amazon.com/dp/B0856VD6TB

Bonus Free Material

If you would like a free book and keep up-to-date with the latest releases, please click on the link below to download:

Subconscious Mind Programming: Unlocking the Tremendous Power of Suggestion

https://bookconnect.review/bookDownload.php?id=1495b6

Also, if you would like a list of free audiobooks, please be sure to Like our Facebook Page and send a message to claim them:

https://www.facebook.com/RylstonePublishing/

Printed in Great Britain
by Amazon